WASHINGTON, DC
Food Crawls

Nomtastic Foods

Getty/iStock/f11photo

TOURING *the* NEIGHBORHOODS
ONE BITE *&* LIBATION *at a* TIME

Globe
Pequot

GUILFORD, CONNECTICUT

Globe
Pequot

An imprint of The Rowman & Littlefield Publishing Group, Inc.
4501 Forbes Blvd., Ste. 200
Lanham, MD 20706
www.rowman.com

Distributed by NATIONAL BOOK NETWORK

All photos by Kimberly Kong unless otherwise noted
Maps by The Rowman & Littlefield Publishing Group, Inc.

British Library Cataloguing in Publication Information available

Library of Congress Cataloging-in-Publication Data available

ISBN 978-1-4930-4510-5 (paper: alk. paper)
ISBN 978-1-4930-4511-2 (electronic)

♾™ The paper used in this publication meets the minimum requirements
of American National Standard for Information Sciences—Permanence of
Paper for Printed Library Materials, ANSI/NISO Z39.48-1992

*Dedicated to fellow foodies who love stuffing their faces
as much as we do. We hope this book helps you find delicious eats
in Washington, DC. Keep up with us on nomtasticfoods.net
for food porn that will leave you hungry for more.*

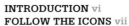

Contents

Introduction

WE STARTED NOMTASTIC FOODS to celebrate our love for delicious eats. There's seriously nothing better than exploring the world and experiencing all the deliciousness it has to offer. Our goal is to fuel your appetite and make sure you always know where and what to devour no matter what you're craving. We've been eating through DC for the past 15 years, and we can't wait to tell you about all the incredible food in the area. We hope you're hungry, and if you're not, you're about to be.

Follow the Icons

 If you eat something outrageous and don't take a photo for Instagram, did you really eat it? These restaurants feature dishes that are Instagram famous. These items must be seen (and snapped) to be believed, and luckily they taste as good as they look!

 Cheers to a fabulous night out in DC! These spots add a little glam to your grub and are perfect for marking a special occasion.

 Follow this icon when you're crawling for cocktails. This symbol points out the establishments that are best known for their great drinks. The food never fails here, but make sure to come thirsty, too!

 This icon means that sweet treats are ahead. Bring your sweet tooth to these spots for dessert first (or second, or third).

 DC is for brunch. Look for this icon when crawling with a crew that needs sweet and savory (or an excuse to drink before noon).

 DC loves its meatless Mondays and meat reduced options. Look for this icon when crawling with vegans and vegetarians in your crew.

THE NAVY YARD CRAWL

1. BLUEJACKET, 300 Tingey St. SE, (202) 524-4862, bluejacketdc.com

2. ANA AT DISTRICT WINERY, 385 Water St. SE, (202) 484-9210, districtwinery.com

3. ICE CREAM JUBILEE, 301 Water St. SE, (202) 863-0727, icecreamjubilee.com

4. RASA, 1247 First St. SE, (202) 804-5678, rasagrill.com

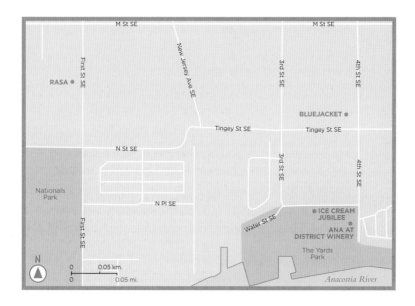

Navy Yard

Home Run Eats

LOCATED ON THE ANACOSTIA RIVER IN SOUTHEAST DC, the Navy Yard has made leaps and bounds since the '90s. It's one of the capital's earliest industrial neighborhoods, and it's now home to the Washington Nationals. Audi Field—home of Major League Soccer's D.C. United—is also close by. You don't have to be a sports fan to have a good time here though. There's always something to do in the Capital Riverfront area!

If you're feeling adventurous, fly high at the Trapeze School NY, or do something a little more low-key like renting a paddleboard at Ballpark Boathouse. Or go ice skating at Canal Park if weather permits. The food scene is booming as well with incredible restaurants like Bluejacket, Osteria Morini, and The Salt Line. If you're a nature lover, there's a ton of green in the area, so take advantage of the beautiful outdoor spaces, and make a note to stop by the bridge at Yards Park for a quick selfie before embarking on your epic food crawl.

1 BLUEJACKET

Chef Marcelle Afram is redefining the meaning of bar food in the capital. Elevated bar food may sound oxymoronic, but you'll understand the hype after dining here. The first thing you'll notice when you walk into BLUEJACKET is the incredible interior. It was built in 1919 as part of the Navy Yard's ship and munitions manufacturing complex, and it's one of the few industrial buildings left in the DC area. Beer lovers will never want to leave the beautiful, pet-friendly patio and the onsite brewery is the cherry on top.

Must-try dishes include their fried mumbo chicken sandwich, their pan-seared pierogis, and their "smother it" tots. The chicken sandwich comes with pickles and coleslaw and is smothered in a ridiculously tasty sauce that was developed in DC in the mid-1900s. Think of it as the District's take on barbecue sauce—it's sweet, tangy and it tastes great with wings, fries, and so much more. The pierogis come with chive reduction, crispy leeks, beech mushrooms, and are filled with charred onion and boursin. And last but not least, their tots are everything and then some. They come with ketchup and dijonnaise, but you can upgrade for $2 and get cheddar and tasso ham gravy.

> When I create the food for the Bluejacket menu, I have the guest in mind. I'm putting myself in their shoes. With thoughtful sourcing, creating, and execution. Beer and food is a communal event. The attempt here is to celebrate that. Delicious and fun things to remember the experience by, that not only make you want to crave a specific beer or food item, but to also crave the experience.
>
> —Marcelle Afram, chef

You honestly can't go wrong with anything you get here, so go wild! Chef Marcelle's always experimenting with new plates, so you know there's always going to be something good on the menu. Come with high expectations and leave completely and utterly satisfied. Bluejacket also does a killer brunch, so make sure you get here bright and early on the weekend! Chef Marcelle's duck confit Benedict and loaded breakfast tots will bring you so much joy.

2 ANA AT DISTRICT WINERY

Next up on the list, a stunning urban winery located along the Anacostia River. Winemaker Conor McCormack produces premium wine in small batches for max deliciousness. You can tour the facility or visit their tasting bar to learn more about their unique process before chowing down at ANA. They have different flight options available (5 wines each) so there's something for everyone.

The restaurant itself is absolutely gorgeous, and the ambiance is second to none. It's flooded with light, and the interior is beautifully decorated. Must-try dishes are as follows: their golden beet *muhammara*, duck wings, and their wild mushroom toast. All three are starters, but they pair beautifully with their vino.

TIP

They have half-price bottle night every Wednesday, so definitely make sure to mark your calendars.

Muhammara is a hot pepper dip that originated in Syria. Ana serves it with frybread, and they top the spread with pomegranate, toasted almonds, Aleppo chiles, and candied lemon. The duck wings are coated in a red curry glaze and are accompanied by a green papaya salad and a side of chef's special aioli. And lastly, the mushroom toast is prepared with hazelnuts and then garnished with shaved parmesan.

Like Bluejacket, they also do a wonderful brunch here, and it's a great place to come with family and friends. Both the *muhammara* and shroom toast are available in the morning as well, but you have to try their cinnamon roll and Dutch apple pancakes because they're absolute staples.

3 ICE CREAM JUBILEE

Take a quick walk to ICE CREAM JUBILEE to satisfy your sweet tooth after chowing down at Bluejacket and Ana. There's a reason why it's so popular—their ice cream is what dreams are made of. They use the best ingredients to create the best product possible. They source their all-natural cream and milk locally and produce everything in small batches to ensure quality. They have crazy creative flavors here, and they're constantly experimenting with cool combinations, so expect to see interesting options when you go.

They have boozy flavors like Banana Bourbon Caramel and Maple Rye Pecan, and their frozen goodies are just the right amount of sweet. They're arguably most famous for

Washington, DC, is a city of passion! People from all over the world are drawn here to create the world that they believe will be the best for their family and future generations. From politicians to activists, to artists and chefs, we all come together with a dream of a better world.

I founded Ice Cream Jubilee after working my dream job on presidential campaigns, in Congress, and as an appointee at the Department of Homeland Security where I helped immigrants in their pursuit of the American Dream. I started Ice Cream Jubilee because I see the world in colors and flavors—I dream in ice cream!

From Passionfruit Guava Sorbet, Mango Habañero, and Citrus Sichuan Peppercorn to Banana Bourbon Caramel and Cookies & Cookie Dough, I channeled my colorful vision of the world into ice cream flavors with the goal of making Washington, DC, and the world a happier place. I'm thrilled that my small business has been received so well—we've been voted Best Ice Cream in DC five years in a row and named one of America's best ice cream shops.

—Victoria Lai, owner

their Thai Iced Tea flavor, and after you try a bite, it won't be difficult to understand why. Get it in a waffle cone for max yumminess and enjoy it by the river if it's nice out.

Also, make sure to give them a follow on Instagram! They have an impressive account with insane dessert creations that will blow your mind and keep you drooling on the regular. You're welcome in advance!

4

RASA

You can't leave Navy Yard without checking out RASA, cofounded by childhood friends Sahil Rahman and Rahul Vinod. Their food is second to none. Think of RASA as an Indian Chipotle . . . except better.

So, here's how it works: You go through a line and pick a base, protein, sauce, and vegetables, and top it with whatever you please. Their basmati rice and lemon turmeric rice are both sublime, but they have other base options like spinach, supergrains, South Indian rice noodles, and more.

If you like lamb, their kebab is the protein for you. It's very flavorful, and the meat melts in your mouth. They also have chicken tikka, spiced beef, turmeric ginger shrimp, sweet potato tikki, green jackfruit, and tofu and cauliflower—lots of options so even the pickiest of eaters can enjoy!

Then comes the sauce—choose from 4 different flavors: tamarind chili, tomato garlic, coconut ginger, and peanut sesame. The tamarind chili

reigns supreme, but you honestly can't go wrong with any of the sauces. Feel free to load your bowl up with various vegetables. Like their sauces, there are 4 options available: charred eggplant, tossed green beans, sauteed spinach, and roasted brussels sprouts.

Finish your creation off with a wide array of toppings. They have so many yum options available, but some popular ones are their cucumber cubes, masala beets, mango salsa, pickled onions, microgreens, and pretty much all of their chutneys. If you're overwhelmed by the choices, they have several pre-made combos to choose from—some winners include their Open Sesame and Aloo Need Is Love bowls.

TIP

On top of bowls, they also offer unique cocktails—think masala gin and tonics and spiked lassis—as well as beer, sides, sweets, and other creative non-alcoholic drinks. Do yourself a solid and get a side of garlic naan, some samosas, and two mango lassis . . . one for the crawl and one for the road.

THE H STREET CORRIDOR CRAWL

1. **FARE WELL,** 406 H St. NE, (202) 367-9600, eatfarewell.com

2. **BEN'S CHILI BOWL,** 1001 H St. NE, (202) 733-1895, benschilibowl.com

3. **POW POW,** 1253 H St. NE, (202) 399-1364, eatpowpow.com

4. **STABLE,** 1324 H St. NE, (202) 733-4604, stabledc.com

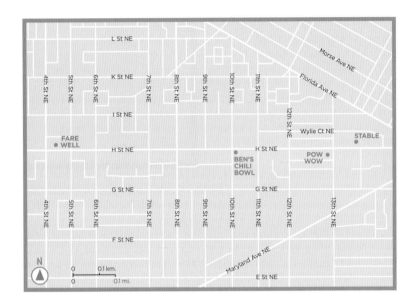

H Street Corridor

H Is for Herbivore

H STREET CORRIDOR WAS FIRST BUILT IN 1849, and it became one of the busiest commercial districts in the capital. Streetcars were built later in the 1870s, and they encouraged growth and helped businesses flourish in the area. Unfortunately, there was a severe decline after World War II, and the 1968 riots left the area in shambles. This prompted revitalization efforts in the early 2000s. It took years to recover, but it's now a mecca for those who seek bustling nightlife and incredible food.

One can enjoy a wide range of cultural activities in the H Street area, home to the Atlas Performing Arts Center and the Rock and Roll Hotel. Whether you want to jam out to indie rock or see flamenco dance, they've got you covered. If it's a beautiful day out, head to Biergarten Haus to enjoy a cold beer with friends. Looking for something cool to do in the p.m.? Check out Little Miss Whiskey's Golden Dollar, a grungy New Orleans-inspired bar, or stop by Copycat Co. to indulge in craft cocktails and dim sum until the wee hours of the morn. The annual H Street Festival is also a great time, with everything from art exhibitions to food trucks. It brings in thousands of people each fall, and local restaurants also like to participate, often creating specials in honor of the occasion.

1

FARE WELL

FARE WELL is DC's first full-service vegan bakery, diner, and bar. When asked about her inspiration behind the concept, chef Doron Petersan said, "when I decided to give up animal products (for the animals, for health, and for the environmental impact), I was sad to give up all of my favorite foods. Growing up in New York (city and upstate) I enjoyed everything, and missed it all desperately. So I decided to try my hand at a few of my favorites."

And try her hand she did. The menu is impressive, boasting a plethora of vegan options that fully satisfy even the pickiest of eaters. The interior's hip; think of it as a trendy '90s diner of sorts. Sit at the bar or grab a table inside or out to enjoy a fabulous meal. Popular plates include their polenta fries, their

> The concept of vegan eating has grown and the fear of all things vegetables has all but died. Fare Well was created to serve the curious carnivore and the hungry open-minded eater. Over the past three years, sales have grown to capacity, and we are busting at the seams, proving that people want to have fun with their food, enjoy something indulgent but healthier, and do so alongside their friends and eating-cohorts.
>
> —Doron Petersan, chef

pierogi appetizer, their southern-fried wings, and any of their baked goods.

Their polenta, served with a side of garlic aioli and tomato jam, is crispy on the outside and creamy on the inside, and it complements their garlic and onion pierogis perfectly. These come with sauerkraut and a dollop of sour cream, and together they make an exceptional bite. Their southern-fried wings are chickpea strips that can be coated in buffalo, mumbo, or barbecue sauce, and they're served with vegetables and a delicious "blue cheese" dipping sauce.

Amazing baked goods are to be expected since Chef Doron's also the owner of Sticky Fingers, a gem of a bakery at 1370 Park Rd NW. She's a two-time winner of Food Network's *Cupcake Wars*, so don't pass on dessert. Fare Well has everything from sticky buns to extravagant layer cakes, and their cookie dough could stop wars.

2 BEN'S CHILI BOWL

No DC food book is complete without a mention of **BEN'S CHILI BOWL**. This District landmark was founded in 1958 on U Street, but it's expanded greatly since then. They now have locations all over the DC area, but Ben's is so much more than just a restaurant. Their establishment celebrates African-American culture. From donating food to Martin Luther King Jr.'s Great March in 1963 to providing shelter to those restoring order after the 1968 riots, they've been a crucial part of the nation's history. Go to their original location on U to take a photo of their elaborate mural on Ben Ali Way, named after their illustrious owner.

In terms of food, they're famous for their Chili Half-Smoke—a half-pork, half-beef dog that's grilled then dressed with mustard, onions, and their spicy homemade chili sauce—but they have several vegetarian options available as well. In fact, their vegan chili's so good that it's received accolades from PETA as well as other organizations.

Indulge in a veggie burger, a veggie burger sub, a veggie dog, or vegan chili for a filling meal that'll satisfy any time of day. They offer both Beyond and Impossible Burger patties, and their chili's made with vegetable protein, green peppers, onions, tomatoes, and kidney beans. They also have hand-spun milkshakes in various unique flavors like cherry, coffee, and maple, and their chili cheese fries are a must-try.

3 POW POW

This trendy fast-casual "new Asian" restaurant fuses Chinese, Japanese, and Korean flavors together to produce unique combinations that will undoubtedly impress. Expect colorful salads, beautiful bowls, and massive egg rolls the size of one's arm. Chef Margaux Riccio and her partner, Shaun Sharkey, source ingredients from local farms whenever possible to ensure quality.

Must-try dishes include their Trolley Fries, their Taiwanese fried mozzarella, and their Natalie Porkman. At $5, their Trolley Fries are a delicious yet affordable treat. They're topped with kimchi, nori, spicy ketchup, *togarashi* mayo, and cashew cheddar. Kimchi is a traditional Korean dish, and many believe it to be vegan, but it actually contains salted seafood called *jeotgal*. Therefore, Chef Margaux's version is less pungent, but it still adds a ton of flavor especially when paired with the aforementioned ingredients.

Her fried "cheese" will leave anyone and everyone speechless. These crispy croquettes are filled with cashew

> I started plant-based cooking for myself. I was hungry, and available "vegan" food wasn't satisfying. Food science allows me to create remarkably close tastes and textures of meat and cheese. Plant protein is the future of food.
>
> —Margaux Cedar,
> executive chef

mozzarella and drizzled with spicy Korean ketchup. They're gooey just like "real" cheese so remember to take a drool-worthy video for Instagram. The Natalie Porkman is one of many customizable bowls available at POW POW, and it contains sweet and sour pork seitan, tomato, grilled pineapple, green pepper, shredded carrots, bean sprouts, and pickled onions. Chef Margaux's "meat" tastes exactly like meat, so expect to be wowed. There's just something about the texture that's exceptional.

Everything on their menu is under $11, and they have several specials available weekly so there's always something new to try. They're closed on Tuesday but open from 11:30 a.m. to 9 p.m. on Monday, Wednesday, and Thursday, and 11:30 a.m. to 10 p.m. Friday through Sunday.

4 STABLE

Unlike Pow Pow, STABLE's not a vegan restaurant, but their raclette is a must-try vegetarian experience when in the District. They have an unlimited option available for brunch and dinner, but reservations are required, and there has to be a minimum of four people. The cheese wheel is prepared tableside, and it's served with boiled potatoes, pickles, salads, and homemade *Wurzelbrot*, a popular Swiss wheat bread that has the appearance of a bumpy tree root due to its unique preparation—it's twisted several times, and it has a sweet crust thanks to its long fermentation process.

Raclette is also available Thursday nights. Get an Instagram-worthy raclette dog, complete with a Frankfurter sausage, homemade bun, and pickles, or go with the deluxe and enjoy melty cheese on potatoes, pickles, and speck. Both dishes are under $10 so they're wallet-friendly options.

Growing up in the Swiss mountains, food played a big role—not only the eating part, but also the planning behind our cuisine.

Our summer is much shorter, but winter lingers around for months, which means all the local farmers had to deal with many months of snow and cold weather. You had to be organized during the spring and summer harvest so you could preserve the spring and summer produce for the cold winter months ahead.

We have a lot of local specialties and every town has its own recipes. A lot of Swiss influences come from our neighbor countries including France, Italy, Austria, and Germany. Swiss food can be best described as a crossroads of flavors from our surrounding neighbors with our own regional and seasonal influences.

—David Fritsche, chef

Although Stable's famous for their raclette, their regular dining menu is also phenomenal. Their whole branzino in salt crust is a masterpiece, and it comes with tomato jam, potatoes, and herb salad. It takes about a

half-hour to prepare this dish for two, but it's well worth the wait. Other standouts include their *Berner rösti* (a potato fritter of sorts, served in a skillet with bits of bacon and onion, topped with gruyère cheese and a fried egg), their beef tartare (minced raw meat with capers, chopped cornichons, shallots, and garlic croutons), and their traditional swiss cheese fondue (3 variations available).

Chef David Fritsche and general manager Silvan Kramer work hard to give their customers five-star dining experiences. They've worked in the industry since they were teenagers, and it was a longtime dream of theirs to open a restaurant together. They're DC's only Swiss-American restaurant, and everything from ambiance to decor is designed to impress. The vibe's upscale even though their price point's quite reasonable. Enjoy brunch from 10:30 a.m. to 2:30 p.m. on Saturday and Sunday, and dinner Tuesday through Saturday from 5:30 p.m. on.

THE CHINATOWN CRAWL

1. REREN, 817 7th St. NW, (202) 209-3677, rerendc.com

2. CHINATOWN EXPRESS, 746 6th St. NW, (202) 638-0424, chinatownexpressdc.com

3. NEW BIG WONG, 610 H St. NW, (202) 628-0491, new-big-wong.com

4. BANTAM KING, 501 G St. NW, (202) 733-2612, bantamking.com

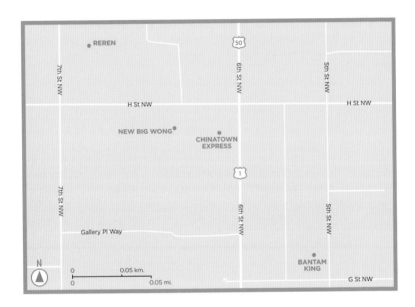

Chinatown

Dim Sum-body Say It's a Food Crawl?

DC'S CHINATOWN MAY NOT BE AS LARGE AS NEW YORK or San Francisco's, but there's still plenty to eat, see, and do. Located east of downtown near Penn Quarter, it's now home to the Washington Wizards and Capitals. Much of this historic neighborhood was demolished in the '90s, but it got a $200 million makeover in 2004. Catch your favorite team in action or come see superstar performers like Beyoncé set the stage on fire at Capital One Arena.

Prefer something a little more low-key? Walk over to the National Portrait Gallery to browse the complete set of presidential portraits or to the Smithsonian American Art Museum to view works from the colonial period to now. If you want to do some high-end window shopping, CityCenter's close by with brands like David Yurman, Dior, and Salvatore Ferragamo. But first things first, head to H and 7th to take a selfie with the iconic Friendship Arch before you get your exploration on.

1

REREN

Located near the Friendship Arch in Chinatown, **REREN**'s known for their dumplings and hand-pulled noodles. They have some of the best spicy wontons in the District, so definitely make sure to get some when you go. They look really spicy because they're drenched in chili oil, but it adds more flavor than heat! In fact, you may actually want to add more chili oil.

Their handmade dumplings are also really good. You get 6 ginormous pieces of perfection with each order, and you have a choice between pork or fish. You can't go wrong with either! The filling's juicy and packed with flavor, and the texture of the wrapper's sublime. They're steamed just right so you won't even care that you can't get them fried.

Since they're also famous for their noodles, you can't leave without getting a bowl or two to share. Their signature "lamen" is a solid choice, but their dan-dan noodles are great if you prefer something without soup. The noodz are amazingly

> Reren goes through 1,140 dumplings per day!

springy, and they come with a ton of toppings. The ground pork is seasoned beautifully, and the peanut-to-noodz ratio is always on point. Mix everything together thoroughly and don't be shy with their bomb chili oil because it elevates anything and everything.

Chef Leopold and his wife make healthy and authentic Asian dishes with no MSG or artificial flavors, so come and indulge guiltlessly. Everything from their noodles to their dumplings are made in-house daily, and their food's affordable so you can come as often as you want without breaking the bank.

2

CHINATOWN EXPRESS

This tiny hole-in-the-wall establishment is known for their noodle soup. Prices are budget friendly, so if you're looking for affordable eats in DC, you're in luck because this is as affordable as they come. You can top your bowl with duck or roast pork, but **CHINATOWN EXPRESS** is famous for duck, so that's the way to go.

If it's too hot for broth, you can always get your noodz stir-fried. They're prepared fresh daily—you can see someone prepping them from the window outside—so you know your meal's going to be solid. The duck is always tender, and the broth is immaculately balanced between salty and umami. If you want to kick things up a notch, add some garlic and chili oil to the soup for a serious flavor explosion in your mouth!

The noodles are on the thicker side—similar to udon—and they're soft yet chewy. They're also known for their dumplings, so make sure you get an order to share. The wrappers are on the doughier side, but some people enjoy that so it's worth a try.

Chinatown Express has been a DC staple for the last 25 years, and their fresh noodle soup with roast duck was voted 2013's "must try dish for every Washingtonian" by readers of the *Washington Post*.

3

NEW BIG WONG

Whether it's noon or midnight, you can always count on **NEW BIG WONG** for delish eats.

This restaurant's a favorite among industry professionals, and many joke that their food tastes better at 2 a.m. Don't let that discourage you from going at a "normal" hour though! Head to this unassuming restaurant for solid Asian comfort food that's great for sharing with friends and fam. They have a huge menu with a lot of Chinese-American options, but skip those and go straight for the following dishes: dry scallop fried rice, crispy roast duck, and snow pea leaves.

If you have trouble finding the magical fried rice on the menu, just tell them you want it when they come for your order. The entree's big enough to feed two to three people, and it contains copious amounts of seafood. It's light and masterfully seasoned. A lot of places overdo it on the soy sauce front, but New Big Wong flavors it just right, and you can taste all the different ingredients.

You always have to get greens for the table, and that's where their snow pea leaves come into play. They're sauteed in garlic, and they have a lovely texture to them. They're dark and leafy and look a lot like spinach. And last but not least, their roast duck. This protein is cooked to crispy perfection, and it's gloriously fatty. Get a half or whole duck depending on how hungry your party is, but watch out for bones.

4

BANTAM KING

Located next to Daikaya, its sister restaurant in Chinatown, **BANTAM KING** is a Japanese noodle shop that specializes in chicken ramen. Chef Katsuya Fukushima crafted a fierce menu, and literally everything on it is gold. Expect killer ramen, bomb fried chicken, and small plates that are almost too tasty to share.

Choose from 5 different ramen flavors: shoyu, miso, spicy miso, shoyu chintan, and veggie. You'd be more than satisfied with any of the afore-mentioned noodz, but their spicy miso's a game-changer. Made with white miso, chili peppers, and peanuts, this complex soup will explode in your mouth in the best way possible. Each bowl's topped with shredded chicken, scallions, mizuna greens, corn, naruto, chili threads, and nori, but you can add whatever your heart desires for a small additional charge.

The fried chicken's an absolute must as well. You can get white or dark meat, and it's served with pickles, white bread, and steamed rice. When they ask if you want to add chicken drippings for a nominal charge, your answer is always yes: no ifs, ands, or buts. Mix all that nomness together for a last meal–worthy dish that will leave you drooling for more. If you're craving spice, make sure to get their gyoza to start. These dumplings look more like wontons, but they're packed with meat, and the chili oil has a serious kick. End your meal on a sweet note with some mochi ice cream and some chicken fat chocolate chip cookies.

THE SHAW CRAWL

1. **SUPRA,** 1205 11th St. NW, (202) 789-1205, supradc.com

2. **ESPITA,** 1250 9th St. NW, (202) 621-9695, espitadc.com

3. **HANUMANH,** 1800 14th St. NW, hanumanh.com

Shaw

Shaw-kingly Delicious Eats

SHAW, ONE OF DC'S OLDEST DISTRICTS, has a very rich African-American history. It's situated east of the U Street Corridor, and it's a hip, up-and-coming area that has a lot to offer. All-star artists perform at the legendary Howard Theatre. Located on what's famously referred to as "Black Broadway," this historic hall was once "the largest colored theatre in the world" as mentioned on their website. It opened in 1910 and presented superstars like Duke Ellington, Ella Fitzgerald, and Nat "King" Cole.

Prefer to indulge in some retail therapy? Head to Steven Alan or venture to the southern section of Shaw to window-shop at CityCenterDC. Enjoy a cold beer with your furry friend at Dacha Beer Garden, then trek to Right Proper Brew Co to snap photos in front of their playful mural art before enjoying a movie at the Atlantic Plumbing Cinema. Afterwards, grab a drink at Columbia Room for a memorable way to end your evening. Located above The Dabney, a Michelin-starred restaurant that specializes in Mid-Atlantic cuisine, this outstanding bar has a tasting menu you won't soon forget. Prefer something a bit more hands on? Book a reservation at Augment Arcade to combine virtual reality gaming with craft cocktails.

1 SUPRA

Welcome to DC's first Georgian restaurant. Since opening their doors in 2017, SUPRA has consistently been awarded Michelin Bib Gourmands. That means for $40 or less, one can enjoy 2 courses and a glass of wine or dessert. Expect phenomenal food that's reasonably priced!

A *supra* is a traditional celebratory feast with an excess of food, drink, and fun, and it's led by the "tamada," a toastmaster whose job is to keep the festivities going. The event is representative of their rich Eastern European culture, showcasing their incredible cuisine and boundless hospitality.

They have strong flavors and impeccable service, and their interior's breathtaking with high ceilings and an open glass concept so the place is flooded with light during the day. In the evening, everything's low lit, making it an ideal date spot. Popular dishes include their tasting board, their *soko ketse*, and their *ajuruli khachapuri*.

The tasting board's wonderful for sharing, and the platter includes several spreads, pickled goodies, cheeses, breads, and more. It comes with an order of eggplant *nigvzit*—rolled eggplant with walnuts and cilantro—which is exceptional.

Soko ketse are stuffed mushrooms. They take cremini mushrooms and fill them with house-made Sulguni cheese. They're baked and come out piping hot, and the cheese is mild enough for everyone to enjoy.

As for entrees, their *khachapuri* is a must. There are 7 different versions available, but the most popular by far is their ajuruli, and this boat-shaped cheese bread is nothing short of life changing. It's topped with an organic egg and a chunk of butter, and it's as scrumptious as it sounds. It's a lot of bread and cheese though, so be prepared to share, and have your phone ready because this dish is arguably one of the most Instagram-worthy plates in the capital.

2

ESPITA

Known for their uber-hip vibe, this modern Oaxacan-inspired restaurant carries over 100 mezcales. Served in 1-, 2-, or 6-ounce pours, they have fantastic options for all price points, and their drinks are served with *sal de gusano* (worm salt) and orange. Worm salt is exactly what one would think it is—salt made with worms. Insects are consumed in over 100 countries, and they're viewed as cheap, sustainable sources of protein. This traditional spice is made with ground agave worms, sea salt, and chiles. It adds a smoky sweetness, and it's commonly used for rimming tequila and mezcal drinks.

ESPITA also has an impressive food menu. They offer non-traditional dishes that pay homage to the flavors of southern Mexico, applying Oaxacan cooking techniques to local ingredients to create inventive dishes. Try their *yuca frita*, their tacos, and their *churros negros*. Their yuca fries are crispy as can be, and they're served with a flavorful chile cream sauce. Squeeze a bit of lime on top to get a nice splash of acidity. They have several tacos available, but popular options include their carnitas and their barbacoa. Conclude your meal with an order of their black churros. They're charred coconut, and they come out warm! They're served with a side of coconut sorbet and dulce de leche ice cream. Who can resist that hot/cold contrast? Soak in the hip interior—complete with stunning mural and all—while savoring each bite.

3

HANUMANH

End the Shaw food crawl on a high note at HANUMANH. Decorated with images of the monkey king, their interior is unique to say the least. The space is cozy, and it has a handful of tables throughout along with bar seating. If weather permits, enjoy food outside on their enclosed patio.

Chef Seng Luangrath is a prominent figure in the Laos food movement, and she runs Hanumanh with her son, chef Boby Pradachith. They're no strangers to the industry, and they already have three wildly successful restaurants under their belts. With Al Thompson, former head bartender at Barmini, running the drink program, they deliver a five-star experience on all fronts, and their recent Michelin Bib Gourmand award comes as no surprise.

They serve small plates that are meant to be enjoyed family style, so

> We do tiki with Lao influence. Promoting the culture of Laos while maintaining a cocktail program that is fun and refreshing that also pairs well with the cuisine. Our goal is to provide a complete experience through communal dining.
>
> —Al Thompson, bar director

go with a group to sample everything and experience the best of Lao cuisine. Their menu's fairly small so that wouldn't be a gluttonous thing to do. Their dishes change frequently depending on what's in season, so there's always something new available. Many of their entrees are gluten free, and they can accommodate vegetarian and vegan requests as well so simply let the waitstaff know.

Must-try dishes are as follows: *sakoo yadsai* (tapioca dumplings with a salted radish-pork-peanut mixture), *cheunh het pouk* (a lightly fried mushroom served with tofu sauce and tamarind salt), and *gaeng phet goong* (red curry prawns with crispy banana blossoms and lychee). As far as drinks go, they have everything from unique sodas to gin cocktails that literally light up. For an Instagram-worthy video, order Al's Romulo in Space. It's a shareable meant for four, and it's made with gin, grapefruit, cinnamon, lime, and pineapple orgeat. It's served in a Storm Trooper helmet and comes complete with Star Wars audio accompaniment.

THE PENN QUARTER CRAWL

1. MOMOFUKU, 1090 I St. NW, (202) 602-1832, ccdc.momofuku.com

2. TEAISM, 400 8th St. NW, (202) 638-6010, teaism.com

3. THE PARTISAN, 709 D St. NW, (202) 524-5322, thepartisandc.com

4. PITANGO GELATO, 413 7th St. NW, (202) 885-9607, pitangogelato
   .com

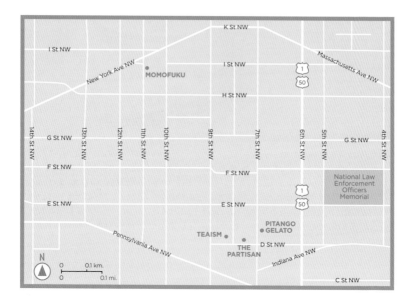

Penn Quarter

Life-Changing Brunch

BETTER KNOWN TO MANY AS OLD DOWNTOWN, Penn Quarter is located in the lower northwest quadrant of DC. This revitalized historic district overlaps with Chinatown at 7th and F, and it is home to all kinds of entertainment. Stop by the Newseum for interactive exhibits that highlight the importance of the free press and the First Amendment or visit the National Building Museum to geek out over architecture and design. Schedule a trip to Ford's Theatre to learn more about President Lincoln's assassination, or if you prefer, go over to Shakespeare Theatre to watch a classic production interpreted through a contemporary lens.

1

MOMOFUKU

Thank the food gods for **MOMOFUKU**. This restaurant opened back in 2015, and it's been going strong ever since thanks to chef Tae Strain and his talented culinary team. They showcase Mid-Atlantic classics alongside Asian staples like Momo Bap, which is a play on bibimbap. This traditional Korean dish literally means "mixed rice," and it usually contains a medley of seasoned veggies, ground beef, and *gochujang* (aka

chili paste). Their delicious take's a definite must-try! It's topped with a poached egg, pickled shiitake mushrooms, and wakame. It comes with a side of *gochujang*, and you can use as little or as much as you'd like.

Their bing bread's also phenomenal, and you can get it with inventive spreads like Path Valley cultured butter with honey and *gochugaru* (aka Korean red pepper powder), pimento cheese with salted chili, bread and butter kohlrabi, and smoked Carolina trout dip with pickled red onion and furikake. The bread looks a lot like naan and comes warm straight out of the oven. And don't forget to save room for dessert because they let you order from Milk Bar— Christina Tosi's famous bakery is adjacent to Momofuku—right at your table. Try their Crack Pie with Cereal Milk soft serve and then get some birthday cake truffles to go for friends. Or for you later.

2

TEAISM

Four words: brunch on a budget. The food at TEAISM is fresh, wholesome, affordable, and most importantly, nomtastic. As you can tell from their name, they're big on tea, but that's not all they do. Their food is second to none, and they have some of the most delectable brunch dishes you'll ever have the pleasure of devouring. Their french toast could stop wars.

This entree alone is worth the visit, and it's available for breakfast Monday through Friday from 7:30 to 11:30 a.m., and Saturday and Sunday from 9:30 a.m. to 2:30 p.m. French toast has never tasted so good. In fact, it's so tasty, you'll let out a satisfied "mmm"

after your first bite. It's topped with stewed apples and cranberries and served with a side of organic maple syrup. You can order 1 slice or 2, but that shouldn't even be a question because your answer is always going to be 2.

After you try their brunch, make it a point to come back for lunch or dinner because there's so much more you need to try. Some favorites include their *okonomiyaki* (Japanese pancake), their South Indian vegetable curry, their udon noodle soup, and their fried chicken bento.

They also have a really interesting section on their menu called "trash or treasure" where they cook up menu items that are typically thrown out. These are the 3 items available: cabbage butts stir fried in *gochujang*, broccoli tots, and seared salmon belly. They're all solid choices, but the broccoli tots are exceptional—you won't even want regular tots after gobbling these babies up. If you go with friends, get

We founded Teaism in 1996 based on a love of the tea leaf. We felt there was a need at the time for people to be exposed to real, high-quality loose leaf teas and we set out to open a teahouse that would serve that purpose. We also wanted people in the United States to understand tea outside of a Western-style, European lens . . . because, surprise, tea is not grown in England! So we wanted to highlight tea's Asian origins. But as restaurant people, we suddenly found ourselves thinking about all the delicious things we could serve with tea in our kitchen at our first location in Dupont Circle. Next thing we knew, Teaism was baking ginger scones, serving up curries and flatbreads, and offering breakfast! That's how we launched into who we are today—a peaceful, laid-back environment to enjoy a good pot of tea and a thoughtful sweet, but also a place where you can get a quick, wholesome, healthy meal.

—Michelle Brown, owner

more than one because there are only 6 per order, and you still want to be friends after your meal. Everything here is made from scratch daily. They even make their own tapioca boba balls from scratch, which is serious dedication.

3 THE PARTISAN

THE PARTISAN can do no wrong. They have some of the best sandwiches in the District, and their brunch offering is straight fire. They're fused with Red Apron, a reputable butcher shop, so they only use the highest quality meats available. Kick your meal off with their pimento cheese appetizer. This Instagram-worthy starter is almost too beautiful to eat. The griddled *tigelles* (traditional Italian bread shaped like disks) are sublime when slathered with gobs of their flavorful spread, so don't pass on this, or their charcuterie.

Now onto the star of the show: their hot wagyu pastrami sandwich. You'll take one look, fall in love, and then die from deliciousness. This massive sandwich is quality at its finest: a crunchy French baguette with huge chunks of smoky, melt-in-your-mouth pastrami, red cabbage slaw, island sauce, and melty swiss cheese. No words can describe this amazing goodness, so you just have to go and try for yourself!

Their Red Apron classic burger is a great choice as well, but you have

> Back when I was the chef at Tallula, we wanted to have a better understanding of where our products were coming from. So I went to the farmers' market and made connections . . . when I asked to buy a New York strip, the farmer told me I needed to buy the hind quarter. That opened the floodgates and we started getting whole pigs, cows, lambs, and goats and utilizing all the pieces into sausages, hams, hot dogs, and charcuterie. Eventually, that side of being a chef consumed me and we wanted to proceed with a concept (shop/store/restaurant) that could feature our goods.
>
> Nathan Anda, chef

to get it with bacon and egg because it's brunch and #treatyourself. They also have a chorizo burger that's dressed with smoked chimichurri, avocado, pickled onions, and sour cream, so if you're feeling adventurous, go with that. They have rotating specials each week so there's always something exciting to try. However, if their pancake burger's available, you'd be doing yourself a disservice by passing, so make sure you get that as well. If you have room, end with their Dutch apple baby! It's made to order, and it's big enough to share with two to three people.

4 PITANGO GELATO

Looking to further indulge your sweet tooth? There's no better way to end a food crawl than with gelato, and PITANGO's frozen treats will leave you wanting more regardless of how full you feel. They epitomize quality to the highest level, and you can really taste the freshness in each bite. Instead of mass producing flavors, they whip up each batch on location. No chemicals, no preservatives, no flavorings: just pure sweet goodness. They also source all their ingredients ethically so you can feel good about where your gelato comes from.

To ensure max deliciousness, they store their flavors in individually sealed compartments to prevent freezer burn or contamination.

They offer unique options like Star Anise, Black Tea, Milk and Honey, and Halvah and Pistachio along with an assortment of sorbets for dairy-free eaters. With flavors like Bosc Pear, Quince, and Rhubarb, you almost want to pass on the gelato and just get sorbet. Overwhelmed by amazing? They give free samples so don't be shy! Get your taste on and see what you like best. They also make some mean pastries, and if you like espresso, their affogato's a must-try!

At Pitango we create gelato and sorbet that embody the flavors of authentic, meticulously curated ingredients. Instead of serving trendy flavors, toppings, and mix-ins, we are purists who celebrate the classics done right.

—Alisa Dan, brand manager

THE DUPONT CIRCLE CRAWL

1. THAI CHEF STREET FOOD, 1712 Connecticut Ave. NW, (202) 234-5698, thaichefdc.com

2. TRIPLE B FRESH, 1506 19th St. NW, (202) 232-2338, triplebfresh.com

3. TIKI TACO, 2010 P St. NW, (202) 986-2121, tikitacodc.com/#home

4. JULIA'S EMPANADAS, 1221 Connecticut Ave. NW, (202) 861-8828, juliasempanadas.com

5. DUKE'S GROCERY, 1513 17th St. NW, (202) 733-5623, dukesgrocery .com

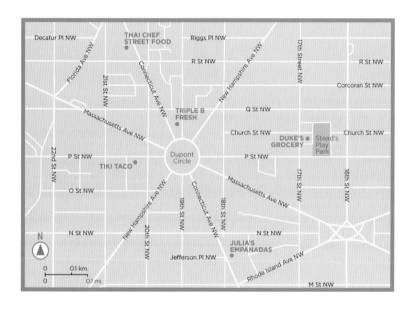

Dupont Circle

Nom-ming on a Budget

DUPONT CIRCLE IS A DIVERSE NEIGHBORHOOD that functions as a hub of culture in DC. Start by walking down Embassy Row, a stretch on Massachusetts Avenue, to see many of the capital's foreign embassies. It is home to diplomatic monuments like the Gandhi Memorial and the Nelson Mandela statue, so have your cameras ready.

If you're an art lover, drive to The Phillips Collection to enjoy contemporary works from masters like Mark Rothko and Georgia O'Keeffe. This ticketed establishment was built in 1941, and it was the first museum for modern art in the United States. They also have a prestigious classical concert series on Sundays featuring world-renowned musicians like Christian Tetzlaff and Nelson Freire.

For a fun night full of laughter, head to DC Improv. It's arguably the most popular comedy club in the city and is definitely worth a visit. Dupont Circle's also known for its nightlife, so if you're ready to dance the night away, add Eighteenth Street Lounge and Heist to your list.

For something a bit more educational, visit the National Geographic Museum on 17th Street. They have everything from exhibitions to lectures to Trivia Night—keep an eye on their calendar to see what's coming up. Finally, no trip to the area would be complete without checking out the Dupont Circle Fountain, so make it a point to go. Grab food and enjoy it there if weather permits or take a quick snap before continuing on with your day of epic eating.

1

THAI CHEF STREET FOOD

Specializing in Bangkok-style street food, **THAI CHEF**'s a welcoming family-run business that's been thriving in Dupont Circle since 2017. Pornnapa Pongpornprot and her eldest daughter Chalisa are passionate about sharing authentic Thai cuisine with DC. The interior's hip, vibrant, and fun, adorned with various decorative pieces straight from Asia.

Everything on their menu is gold, but standout dishes include their *kao mun gai* and their papaya salad. *Kao mun gai* is a traditional Thai street food of steamed chicken served over jasmine rice. It's accompanied by sliced cucumbers, cilantro, and spicy garlic ginger sauce, which sounds simple, but the flavor profile's quite complex. The combination of the chicken, garlic, and herbed rice is explosive. The papaya salad is yet

another hit, and it has sliced green papaya that's pounded with garlic, tomatoes, roasted peanuts, basil leaves, fresh lime juice, and hot pepper. This gluten-free dish packs quite a punch, so keep a glass of water nearby.

On top of delicious food, they have imaginative cocktails using ingredients like lemongrass, tamarind, and more. They also have a delightful dessert bar with Instagram-worthy desserts like mango sticky rice, egg waffles, and crispy banana ice cream.

> When people step in our restaurant, I want them to feel like they're at a night market in Bangkok, with the ambiance with bright colors and neon signs, our Bangkok street food menu that my family and I grew up eating, and our specialty cocktails.
>
> —Chalisa Fitts, co-owner

2 TRIPLE B FRESH

If you haven't tried *kimbap* yet, you need to because it's a game-changer. This popular Korean dish is a rice roll that typically contains meat and an assortment of colorful vegetables. *Kim* means seaweed and *bap* means rice, and it is street food that's known for its portability and deliciousness. Although good Korean food is hard to come by in the District, you can get a lovely taste at **TRIPLE B FRESH**, all under $10.

You have a choice between 5 different rolls: classic, *bulgogi*, tuna, kimchi, and veggie. All are tasty, but if you're a meat-eater, definitely try the *bulgogi*. It translates to "fire meat" in English, and it's marinated slices of beef that's stir-fried or barbecued. The roll also contains crabstick, pickled radish, watercress, carrots, cucumber, pickled squash, and egg. It's thinly sliced so each piece is the perfect bite!

They also specialize in bibim-bap, which means "mixed rice." They have over 30 toppings available, and they make everything fresh daily so you know you're getting quality. You can get a pre-made bowl or build your own with white, black, or brown rice. If you're not sure what flavors will go together best, get the classic in a stone pot, otherwise known as *dolsot*, with a fried egg on top.

On top of the aforementioned staples, they also offer other Korean favorites like *ddukbokki* (spicy rice cakes) and *japchae* (stir-fried glass noodles with thinly sliced vegetables). The restaurant itself is located down a flight of stairs, but there's seating both inside and outside.

3 TIKI TACO

Chef Ryan Fichter brought a bit of Hawaii to DC with TIKI TACO, located in an unassuming space on P Street. He lived there for several years before moving to the capital and found himself longing for the local cuisine he fell in love with. He fuses island flavors into his food, creating inventive bites that will captivate your taste buds.

This down to earth, order-at-the-counter restaurant's known for their tacos, poke bowls, wings, and shaved ice. Fichter is not trying to offer traditional Hawaiian food but rather innovative flavor combinations that pay homage to the cuisine. He says: "When I was conceptualizing this restaurant, I wanted to do something different. I didn't want to be just another run of the mill taco joint. So, I thought to myself what can I do that is recognizable enough for people to try, but different enough to match my personality and tastes in food. I think it was at this point that I had my 'aha' moment . . . Island Style Tacos! I was going to draw inspiration from my time in Hawaii and traveling the islands to influence my food. I said, 'wow it's never been done before and that is how I can make my mark!' So, I set forth to create my own niche in the taco game."

Get a trio of 3 tacos for $9.75 or a single for $3.50. Some popular options include their pork belly (dressed with cabbage kimchi, tomato, avocado, and shoyu glaze), their crispy sesame tofu (topped with green papaya salad, toasted coconut, and sweet chili sauce), and their Kailua pork (topped with watercress and pineapple salsa).

If you're craving seafood, you're in luck because they do poke so well. Choose between ahi tuna or salmon and get it prepared three different ways: traditional, shoyu, and tiki style. It's hard to pick favorites, but shoyu

Good food for me is a balance of clean flavors and proper technique. You don't need a ton of ingredients to make a dish taste good. Just start with the best fresh ingredients, use proper technique, salt, and 99 percent of the time you will create something deliciously yummy! As for that other 1 percent, well no one is perfect: just learn from it and don't be afraid to try new things.

—Ryan Fichter, chef

is always a great choice. The sauce is made with Maui sweet onions, scallions, soy sauce, and sesame. Their jerky blue wings are fantastic as well, but their spiced pineapple glaze could move mountains. Get 9 for $10, and remember to get a shaved ice to share. They have a huge assortment of syrups, so take advantage and get a rainbow-flavored one. Not only is it enjoyable to eat, it's great for photos as well!

4 JULIA'S EMPANADAS

JULIA'S is DC's very first empanada restaurant, and it was established in 1993. They got so popular that they opened two other locations in the capital—one in Adams Morgan and one in Brightwood. All their food is "made with love," and their empanadas are baked fresh daily so the dough's always wonderfully chewy. They offer various different flavors, but their Chilean-style and chorizo are popular choices. They also have a vegetarian option available each week.

The Chilean-style empanada contains beef, raisins, egg, olives, onions, and a medley of aromatic spices, while the chorizo's made with Spanish sausage, black beans, rice, and onions. These magical pockets of goodness are stuffed to the brim, and they're shockingly filling. The pastry's nice and flaky, and its crispiness contrasts beautifully with the savory quality of the meat. To take things up a notch, ask for some of their secret hot sauce. It's very flavorful and adds a good amount of heat. They also offer salads and homemade soups along with delightful dessert empanadas like pineapple coconut and peach guava.

5 DUKE'S GROCERY

There's a reason why everyone raves about DUKE'S GROCERY; the hype is justified. They have three restaurants in Washington, but the Dupont location's the original. The interior's unique because it's a historic row house with two floors and a patio. They've been voted best burger in DC year after year, and you'll understand why once you try their Proper burger. It's made with locally sourced Angus beef then topped with melted gouda and pickled charred red onion. It's dressed with sweet chili sauce and garlic aioli and served on a buttery brioche bun. The meat's juicy as can be, and the burger's sweet, savory, and salty all at the same time.

Other standout dishes include their truffle mac and cheese, and their local *elote locos*. The mac is big enough to share among two or three people, and the truffle's distinct but doesn't overpower. The plate is incredibly rich, and the broiled cheese on top has an excellent texture to it. The *elote* is seasoned phenomenally, and it contains charred sweet corn with *crema mexicana*, Cotija cheese, red chili, and lime. This dish has so much zing; it's like a flavor explosion in your mouth. They also have a generous happy hour from 12 p.m. to 7 p.m. Monday through Friday, so make sure you take advantage of their $6 beers, wines, and liquors.

THE COLUMBIA HEIGHTS CRAWL

1. **MEZCALERO COCINA MEXICANA,** 3714 14th St. NW, (202) 803-2114, mezcalerodc.com

2. **PHO VIET,** 3513 14th St. NW, (202) 629-2839, phovietwdc.com

3. **THIP KHAO,** 3462 14th St. NW, (202) 387-5426, thipkhao.com

4. **BOMBAY STREET FOOD,** 1413 Park Rd. NW, (202) 758-2415, bombaystreetfood.us

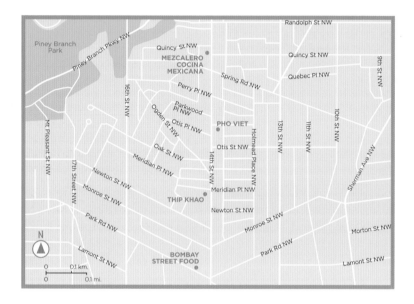

Columbia Heights

Diversifying Your Palate

KNOWN FOR MULTICULTURAL VIBES, COLUMBIA HEIGHTS has a very diverse food scene with everything from Laotian to Filipino cuisine. Located north of Adams Morgan, it's one of DC's most densely populated neighborhoods. Work up an appetite by renting a bike from Capital Bike-share to explore the area and view modern architecture along with historic 19th-century buildings. Then walk down 11th or 14th Street for incredible eats that will blow your mind.

Visit during the weekend from April to December to experience their local farmers' market and enjoy live music, fresh produce, and delicious noms. Or you could head to the GALA Hispanic Theatre to see one of the oldest Spanish-language groups in action. Don't worry, they have English translations going on simultaneously so you'll be able to follow along with ease! You could also stop by Meridian Hill Park for a low-key afternoon of R&R before checking out the Mexican Cultural Institute. This 20th-century complex used to be the Mexican Embassy, but now this museum hosts everything from concerts to cooking classes.

1

MEZCALERO COCINA MEXICANA

When you think of incredible tacos, DC's probably not the first city that comes to mind, but there's some seriously yummy Mexican food in the capital. Chef Alfredo Solis and his sister Jessica opened MEZCALERO COCINA MEXICANA to bring authentic and affordable noms to the District, and they've been killing it since day 1. Chef makes all his food from scratch, so you know you're getting serious quality regardless of what you get.

His tacos are only $2.50 to $3 dollars apiece, so you can get a ton of bang for your buck here. There are 15 different kinds, so make sure you come back and try them all. They're served on handmade corn tortillas, but

you can get flour ones if you prefer. Try getting the chorizo and tinga to start. They smell like heaven, and they taste even better. Chorizo's spicy sausage with onions and cilantro and the tinga's chicken that's marinated in the most flavorful of chipotle sauces, served with lettuce, queso fresco, and sour cream.

On top of a dope food menu, they carry 60 different kinds of mezcal, so come with your friends for a good time all around.

There are a handful of solid vegetarian options as well, so rest assured, there's something for everyone. Their *huitlacoche* quesadilla—made with Mexican corn truffle, cheese, and avocado—is a definite crowd pleaser. Now, you're probably wondering what *huitlacoche* is. "Mexican corn truffle" sounds fancy, but it's actually a plant disease that grows on corn and looks like stones. It tastes earthy like mushrooms with a cooked corn texture, and it's a delicacy that many savor, so go and try for yourself. His enchiladas are also really tasty—try *el pollo* with some spicy salsa drizzled on top and cool down your tongue with a refreshing glass of horchata.

2 PHO VIET

A good bowl of pho isn't something you find easily in DC, which is why you should be dog-earing this page right about now. PHO VIET has been serving authentic Vietnamese food in the area for the last 10 years, and they're known for their incredible broth. Located on the ground floor of a Columbia Heights row house, this hole-in-the-wall gem will leave you totally content. Ambiance isn't their strong suit, and there's limited seating available, so expect to eat family style.

They're famous for their spicy lemongrass pho, but their regular is tasty as well. Each bowl is served with a side of uber-fresh bean sprouts, jalapeños, basil, and lime, and there's a vegetarian option which comes with tofu, broccoli, cauliflower, and carrots. You choose from 10 different meat combinations—all available in regular or large sizes—but their beef special is the way to go. They also do a mean vermicelli bowl! You can't go wrong with any of their proteins, but they hit it out of the park with their honey

lemongrass pork and crispy egg roll combo. And don't forget to start your meal off with a Vietnamese coffee and an order of summer rolls—they're as fresh as can be, and they come with the nuttiest peanut sauce.

3 THIP KHAO

Chef Seng Luangrath and her son, chef Bobby Pradachith, take Lao cuisine to a whole 'nother level with THIP KHAO. They're heavy-handed with spice so their food is bold and flavorful. If you're not an adventurous eater, this is a stellar opportunity for you to branch out and try something new. Their jungle menu has special proteins like chicken heart, pig ear, and minced alligator, so go wild. Crowd-pleasers include their *khao poon*, *muu som*, and *moak paa*.

You can get their *khao poon* with catfish, chicken, or tofu, and it's probably the most delicious red curry you'll ever have. Think awesome vermicelli noodles in a decadent broth that's large enough to feed at least two people. The *muu som* is rice-cured sour pork belly, and it's served with wood ear mushrooms, puffed rice, toasted chiles, and other magical spices. It's a very rich dish with meat so tender, it falls apart in your mouth. The *moak paa* is like a Laotian tamale of sorts, and you can get it with salmon, catfish, or mushrooms. Your choice of protein is steamed inside banana leaves along with rice paste, mushrooms, and coconut, and you will want to

dip your sticky rice inside that goodness for a flavor explosion that will always leave you completely satisfied. Other popular dishes include their papaya salad and their *laab* (a type of meat salad). Get the latter with duck to start your meal off with a bang!

4

BOMBAY STREET FOOD

If you're looking for solid Indian food in Columbia Heights, you're in for a serious treat, so loosen your belt buckles. The first thing you'll notice when you walk in the door at BOMBAY STREET FOOD is their brilliant decor. The restaurant has a vibrant atmosphere with colorful walls that are covered with photographs of Bollywood stars, impressive Indian landmarks, and more. Asad Sheikh, co-owner and award-winning restauranteur, is no stranger to the industry. He's opened several top-notch restaurants in Northern Virginia (London Curry House, 1947, and Curry Mantra), so you know he has the necessary tools to deliver an outstanding dining experience.

Their menu's large so there's a lot to choose from, and they have everything from street food staples to Indo-Chinese dishes. Some must-trys include their chicken tikka roll, their paneer pakora, their chicken biryani, and their Bombay thali dinner.

Their roll, also known as the Frankie, contains chicken tikka, egg, and a delish ginger-garlic chutney. You can also get it with sheek kebab or paneer if you prefer. Their paneer pakora (deep-fried cheese) is a part of their "monsoon" menu, and each order comes with an oh so flavorful cup of cutting chai. What's not to like? They do sweet and savory so well!

The biryani is big enough to share with at least one other person, and you can get it with chicken, lamb, or shrimp. It comes out steaming hot, capped with a naan-like pastry, and the spices used are incredible. The meat is succulent, and the aromatic rice will leave you wanting more regardless of how full you are. Now, if you're looking to sample a bunch of different dishes, you have to get their Bombay thali dinner. They say it feeds two people, but you could easily feed a group with all the food they give you.

THE ADAMS MORGAN CRAWL

1. AMSTERDAM FALAFELSHOP, **2425 18th St. NW, (202) 234-1969,** falafelshop.com

2. BUL, **2431 18th St. NW, (202) 733-3921, buldc.com**

3. MEZE, **2437 18th St. NW, (202) 797-0017, mezedc.com**

4. DONBURI, **2438 18th St. NW, (202) 629-1047, donburidc.com**

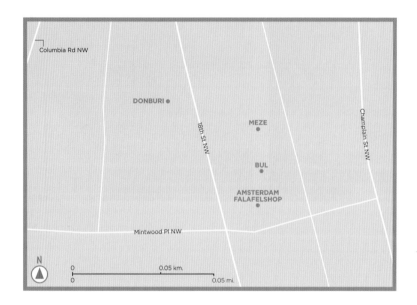

Adams Morgan

Satisfy Late-Night Cravings

ADAMS MORGAN IS, HANDS DOWN, ONE OF THE HIPPEST neighborhoods in the capital. It's located north of the White House, and it's lined with historic row houses that are beautifully maintained. This diverse community has a surplus of unique shops, bars, and restaurants, so there's always something to do. Check out Meeps for vintage threads, Urban Dwell for eccentric gifts, and Commonwealth for dapper menswear. Stop by Idle Time, a two-story used bookstore that's been around since 1981, to browse their massive collection of 50,000 books before heading to The LINE hotel for a cool photo opp. The building channels quintessential DC, and it was built inside a 110-year-old church so there's a lot of history behind the architecture.

In the mood for some family-friendly entertainment? Go to the District of Columbia Arts Center to enjoy everything from improv comedy to contemporary art exhibitions. A trip to Adams Morgan wouldn't be complete without experiencing their infamous nightlife. Madam's Organ is one of the oldest establishments in the area, and there are 5 different bars inside with live music daily. Finish your night on a high note by visiting the many restaurants that are open until the wee hours of the night.

1 AMSTERDAM FALAFELSHOP

"Don't forget to crush your balls!" This strange but hilarious phrase is commonly heard at **AMSTERDAM FALAFELSHOP** because their magical chickpea goodness tastes better when smushed and dispersed. This vegan-friendly fast-casual joint has a small but mighty menu that's packed with a ton of flavor. Choose between a falafel pita sandwich or a salad bowl, and get a side of fries with curried ketchup and garlic cream sauce.

Their pita is available in two different sizes: the small comes with 3 falafel, the large with 5. Get either white or wheat—the former's more flavorful than the latter—and load up on condiments at their all-you-can-eat topping bar. It's self-serve so feel free to go a second time with the cups they provide. They have over 20 toppings

with everything from chickpea salad to creamy coleslaw.

Their falafel is crunchy on the outside and fluffy on the inside. Their sandwiches are easy to eat and have wonderful portability. The restaurant itself has an urban vibe to it, and there are a handful of cafe tables available in addition to counter seating. It's the best way to start a late-night food crawl in Adams Morgan.

2 BUL

Bul means fire in Korean, and it's a great name for this fantastic restaurant that specializes in Asian street food. Think of **BUL** as DC's version of a Korean *pojangmacha* (often abbreviated as "pocha"), a tented area that offers affordable but delicious bites like *kimbap*, rolled korean "sushi," and *ddukbokki*, spicy rice cakes. They're open late into the night, which means lots of *soju* (a Korean alcoholic beverage), lots of food, and lots of fun.

They have everything from *budae jjigae* (a Korean stew) to Korean tacos, and their menu's huge so there's a lot to choose from. Popular dishes include their *rabokki*, their o-crab puffs, and their K.F.C. *Rabokki* is a combination of *ddukbokki* and ramen, and it's served in

a spicy red pepper sauce with fish cakes and scallions. It has a decent kick to it, and the portion's huge so sharing is a must! Their puffs are crispy morsels of goodness stuffed with cream cheese, crab, and green onion, served in a sweet and sour dipping sauce.

Don't fill up though because their K.F.C is easily the star of the show. They have some of the best Korean fried chicken in the capital, and it is prepared extra crispy on the outside and extra juicy on the inside. Ask for a side of *bul* sauce if you can handle heat, and enjoy both flavors like a pro. Service here is always prompt, and their price point's reasonable so expect to be back soon.

3

MEZE

Located in the heart of Adams Morgan, MEZE is one of the oldest restaurants in the area. They've been serving delicious Turkish specialties to DC residents since 2001, and they're known for their outstanding food and lovely ambiance. The restaurant takes its name from *meze*, which are essentially the Eastern Mediterranean equivalent of Spanish tapas. They're intended for sharing, and they allow diners to experience various flavors throughout their meal.

They're famous for their mojitos, so definitely take advantage of their being half off. Imported beers are available for $4 and rail drinks and wine for $5 a glass. They also have a special food menu with $5 plates. There's a lot to choose from, including a handful of vegan/vegetarian options, so go with a large group of friends and share.

Popular dishes are as follows: *tavuk kofte* (chicken meatballs), vegetarian *sigara böregi* (cigar-shaped pastries filled with feta), vegan *dolma* (stuffed grape leaves) and their *cerkez tavugu* (shredded chicken dip with walnuts accompanied by homemade bread). They also have a delightful family-style menu featuring 11 different items for $35 a person if you prefer. Whatever you choose, just remember to end your meal on a sweet note with an order of their *kunefe*. It's a traditional dessert "pancake" made from wheat, cheese, and crushed pistachios, and it's served piping hot with lemon syrup. The perfect end to a perfect meal.

4 DONBURI

DONBURI is Japanese comfort food at its finest. The word itself means "rice bowl dish," and the translation's quite straightforward since it's a bowl of white rice topped with different proteins, sauces, and garnishes. Choose from a variety of signature offerings, salads, and curry *donburi*. Their *sakedon* is a must for sashimi lovers—think high-quality salmon that's buttery as can be, served with an assortment of pickled vegetables and fresh wasabi. The rice is seasoned with *katsuobushi* (dried fish) extract, and the flavors complement the fatty fish beautifully.

Craving meat? Get their *karaagedon* instead, and choose between Japanese curry or traditional *donburi* style. The fried chicken's marinated in soy sauce, and the meat's as juicy as can be. The pickled toppings provide great textural contrast, and the bowl comes with a runny egg. Order a side of *ebi katsu* to share, and enjoy the crispy magic of their panko-coated shrimp.

The restaurant itself has a very cozy feel with limited bar seating around the kitchen. It's usually busy and everything's made to order, so expect a wait. Pay before you sit down to eat and remember to get some sake or plum wine to accompany your meal.

THE WHARF CRAWL

1. FALAFEL INC, 1140 Maine Ave. SW, (202) 488-4983, falafelinc.org

2. GRAZIE GRAZIE, 85 District Sq. SW, (202) 216-2999, graziegrazie.com

3. KITH/KIN, 801 Wharf St. SW, (202) 878-8566, kithandkindc.com

4. TOASTIQUE, 764 Maine Ave. SW, (202) 484-5200, toastique.com

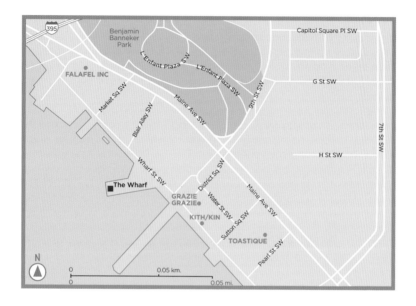

The Wharf

Dining by the Water

Located along the Potomac, the Wharf is one of the hottest areas in Washington, DC. Home to over 20 trendy restaurants and bars, it's only a few blocks away from the National Mall. There are tons of family-friendly activities available, so it's a wonderful place to go with kids. Spend the day at one of their parks—choose between 7th Street, Waterfront, and Banneker, or visit all three—before enjoying dinner by the water. If the weather's nice, kayak or paddleboard in the river or take their free jitney to explore East Potomac Park.

For live entertainment, head to The Anthem for an experience of a lifetime. This incredible music hall can fit anywhere from 2,500 to 6,000 people, and they feature artists from all musical genres including megastars like Lizzo and Zedd, and the National Symphony Orchestra. Prefer something a bit more intimate? Go to Pearl Street Warehouse for a more relaxed show.

From November to February, the Wharf has a lovely cash-free ice rink next to the Transit Pier that's open to the public. You can rent skates onsite or bring your own. Lastly, make sure you visit the municipal fish market before you leave. It's the country's oldest open-air fish market, so remember to get some fresh seafood to share.

1

FALAFEL INC

The falafel at FALAFEL INC have a fantastic texture, and sandwiches are only $3 a pop. They're fried to order and they come with lettuce, red cabbage, *pali* salad, *tatbili*, tahini, and red sauce on a freshly baked pita. Spend an extra dollar to get a salad bowl instead, and get a heaping bowl of greens with red cabbage, tabouli, tomato, cucumber, pickles, and za'atar chips, topped with their special house dressing. They source their ingredients locally so their food's as fresh as can be, and they make everything from scratch using secret family recipes so there's love in each bite.

There are 8 sides available including hummus and cucumber salad; however, the standout by far is their za'atar fries. Za'atar is a Middle Eastern spice blend that's commonly used as a condiment, and it contains herbs

and spices such as toasted sesame seeds and dried sumac. They season their crispy fries heavily, but the flavor's just right, and it tastes great when dipped in their signature Habibi Sauce. They have 5 other sauces available though, so sample them all to see which one tastes best.

The restaurant's goal is to feed a million refugees per year, and they're well on their way with new stores opening in Los Angeles, Mexico City, Dubai, Boston, and more. They want to build a worldwide community of more than 100 restaurants and encourage eating for good. For every $10 spent, they donate food to feed a refugee for a day.

Their new space at the Wharf opened in the spring of 2019, and it's bigger than their location in Georgetown. Like their flagship, this restaurant doesn't have indoor seating, but they have tables set up outside, and there's plenty of seating by the water, which is a better view anyway. Service is quick, and Falafel Inc is easily one of the most affordable and delicious food options in the area—if not the entire city—so go and indulge.

2 GRAZIE GRAZIE

This fast-casual sandwich joint is anything but average. GRAZIE GRAZIE may be one of the less expensive options in the neighborhood, but the flavors are 200 percent there, which makes the price point all the sweeter. The restaurant has a relaxed urban vibe, and the atmosphere's upbeat. Service is always friendly and efficient, and their enthusiasm's infectious.

They have a fairly large menu with hot and cold gourmet subs, salads, starters, and desserts, and popular choices include their *russoniello*, their *nonna*, their *minelli*, and their risotto balls. They also have a great selection of vegetarian and vegan options, and customization's available as well. Order at the counter and quickly take a seat because this place gets packed during peak hours, and tables are limited.

The *russoniello* contains house roast pork, broccoli rabe, and mounds of shredded sharp provolone. It's finished with a drizzle of extra virgin olive oil, and it's almost too beautiful to eat. The *nonna* is their meatball sub, and

it's topped with melted provolone, marinara, sliced pepperoncini, and basil leaves. Come hungry because it's very filling.

Craving the ultimate cold cut sub? The *minelli*'s made with hot capicola, peppered ham, and prosciutto. The bread's slathered with spicy aioli and filled with oven-dried tomatoes and red onions. The sandwich is then topped with arugula, basil, and house seasoning before getting a drizzle of olive oil and red wine vinegar. Portions here are huge, so share with a friend or save half for another meal. They don't skimp on meat and only use high-quality ingredients that satisfy, so expect serious bang for your buck.

Still hungry? Their risotto balls are lightly fried bites of heaven. They're gooey on the inside, so have your camera ready for a fabulous cheese pull that will feed everyone's feed. Enjoy them with a side of their hearty marinara sauce.

3 KITH/KIN

KITH/KIN gets a lot of love from the DC community. Chef Kwame Onwuachi is a James Beard Rising Star winner and former *Top Chef* contender, so, suffice it to say, he brings a lot of press. Through his food, he celebrates his culture and highlights his roots, showcasing flavors from Nigeria to the Caribbean and everywhere in between. It's worth a visit to try his menu, but this crawl focuses on their dessert offerings.

Executive pastry chef Paola Vélez has worked with prominent figures like Jacques Torres and Christina Tosi, and prior to joining the team at Kith/Kin, she was at Iron Gate. She demonstrates her mastery with treats like her lemon puff puff, rum cake, and chocolate chip thick'em. Think of her puff puff as a Nigerian beignet of sorts. It's exceptionally fried, and the

> My grandmother radically influenced who I am as a cook today. We had a lot of land, but we weren't well off. The land was called El Cacao which just means the cocoa trees. In between the cocoa we had multiple fruit trees, plantain, herb gardens, even coffee. We used those resources to cook on a wood fire to feed the neighborhood. At noon, everyone came to enjoy Mama Paulina's cooking. Inspired by Mama, I want to always emulate that sense of community and love. To cultivate memories on a plate to transport the diners' experience with my food.
>
> —Paola Vélez, executive pastry chef

dough is as soft as can be. It's served with a side of passion fruit curd that adds just the right amount of sweet.

The rum cake is large enough for two to three people, and it's made with an eight-year Bacardi. The dessert is topped with chocolate crumble, and the texture is out of this world. Her chocolate chip cookie contains Tainori dark chocolate, Jivara milk chocolate, and butterscotch. This is no ordinary cookie. The size itself is staggering, and it has layers of goodness inside. So end the Wharf crawl on a high note with world class desserts at Kith/Kin. Soak in the incredible ambiance and savor each decadent bite.

4

TOASTIQUE

Founder Brianna Keefe dreamed of having her own health cafe for years, and now she has two: one in the Wharf and one in Old Town Alexandria. As a serious Division I athlete, Keefe was always passionate about fitness and nutrition. She wanted to deliver nourishing food without sacrificing taste or presentation, and at TOASTIQUE, she did exactly that. The menu's straightforward with a variety of mouthwatering options. Choose from gourmet toasts, cold-pressed juices, wholesome smoothies, collagen iced lattes, and stunning acai bowls.

The decor's trendy, complete with a plant wall, yet unpretentious. It's another fast-casual joint, but the atmosphere is on the more sophisticated side. Their toasts are served on wooden boards that ooze classy rustic vibes, and each combination is gorgeous in its own right. Some of the more popular toasts include their avocado smash, their smoked salmon, and their PB crunch.

The smash is multigrain toast topped with a generous amount of avocado and marinated tomatoes, then garnished with watermelon radish and microgreens. It's drizzled with chili oil and a sprinkle of toasty seasoning to finish things off. The salmon comes on sourdough toast, and it's served with thinly sliced cucumbers and herb cream cheese. The brininess of the capers complements the richness of the cream cheese. Get it with a poached egg for yolk porn at its finest! The last toast is sweet rather than savory. This fruit-centric dish is served on raisin walnut toast and is topped with honey-roasted peanut butter, sliced bananas and strawberries, granola, honey, chia seeds, and some mint. Although each creation is loaded with toppings, the bread stays nice and crispy. Prefer something lighter? Keep things simple and get a juice to cleanse your palate.

THE CAPITOL HILL CRAWL

1. **BARREL,** 613 Pennsylvania Ave. SE, (202) 543-3622, barreldc.com

2. **JOSELITO,** 660 Pennsylvania Ave. SE, (202) 930-6955, joselitodc
   .com

3. **MATCHBOX,** 521 8th St. SE, (202) 548-0369, matchboxrestaurants
   .com

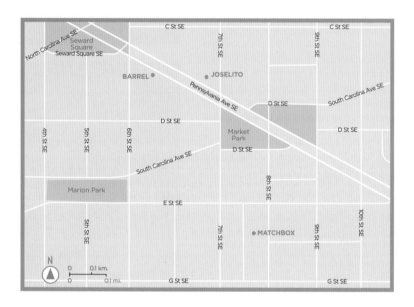

Capitol Hill

Power Brunch It Up

WHETHER YOU WANT TO SEE CONGRESS IN ACTION or enjoy a beautiful Michelin Star meal, the Hill has you covered. Start with a free 90-minute tour of the US Capitol before heading to the Library of Congress to browse their impressive collection. This massive building was built in 1897, and it's home to over 164 million items. Enjoy the stunning Italian Renaissance–style architecture before heading to your next destination.

A visit to the Botanic Garden is a must. With over 28,000 square feet of plant life, it's a free attraction at the base of Capitol Hill that's open 365 days a year. One of the highlights there is their conservatory, and it has 10 different rooms along with two courtyard gardens. There's a lot to see, but their orchid room's a standout. Also make sure to walk around their National Garden. It is 3 acres of pure beauty featuring plant life from all over the United States.

If you prefer live entertainment, go see a play or concert at the Folger Shakespeare Library before walking to Eastern Market to browse fresh produce and crafts. The latter was completed in 1873 and was considered the "town center" for decades. In 2007, the market experienced severe damage by fire, but the government restored it to its glory in 2009, and it's thriving yet again. Go on a Saturday or Sunday to purchase everything from handmade jewelry to vintage threads, and see what DC artisans have to offer.

1

BARREL

There's a reason why **BARREL** is packed at 10:45 a.m. on a Saturday morning. Washingtonians are serious about brunch, and who can blame them when there's incredible food and bottomless make-your-own mimosas. Established in 2014, this sophisticated neighborhood bar has an impressive barrel aging program, and their craft cocktails are a must.

Indulge in southern-inspired dishes that are all made from scratch, and enjoy a drink or two. Popular brunch plates include their mac and cheese, their tagliatelle alla carbonara, and

their fried chicken. Their mac and cheese is crisp on the outside and creamy on the inside, but it's very rich so get it to share. Their tagliatelle alla carbonara is everything one could hope for. Think thick chunks of bacon in a luscious cream sauce with chewy noodles topped with a poached egg. Prefer something different? Try their fried chicken. It's tender and moist, and served with a biscuit and doused with red eye gravy.

Brunch wouldn't be brunch without mimosas. Their Instagram-worthy drink bucket comes fully equipped with OJ, cranberry juice, seasonal syrups, and a bottle of champagne. There's a 2-hour limit, but that's still plenty of time to do some damage and start your Capitol Hill crawl off with a bang.

2 JOSELITO

With chef David Sierra at the helm, JOSELITO is flourishing with its unique take on traditional Spanish cuisine. This Michelin Bib Gourmand awarded restaurant serves weekend brunch from 10:30 a.m. to 3 p.m. They have a separate menu for the occasion, but they still serve everything from their regular a la carte menu.

Start with an order of their Jamon Ibérico de Bellota "Capanegra." This hand cut Iberian ham goes beautifully with Manchego cheese, and it's a great way to kick off your meal. Follow up with a bowl of their *sopa de coliflor trufada con panceta y gamba*, a truffled cauliflower soup with pork belly and shrimp. Squeeze the head to get max flavor, and savor the deliciousness that ensues. Move onto a beautiful salad course with their *remolacha con queso fresca y manzana verde*. This amazing beet goodness is served with uncured buffalo cheese, sliced green apples, fennel, and onion and is dressed with a light sherry vinaigrette.

Your meal wouldn't be complete without trying their *pasta con txangurro, erizo de mar*, egg pasta with jumbo crab meat and sea urchin served with shrimp butter. It's bucatini with rosemary undertones that's as creamy as can be. This is buttered pasta at its finest, and it's rich but not overwhelmingly so.

Joselito offers most everything in the following sizes: *tapa*, *media ración*, and *ración*. They also have a bottomless mimosa, Bellini, sangria, and Bloody Mary bar available. Purchase drinks by the glass or indulge in an unlimited deal to enjoy with your meal.

3 MATCHBOX

End this Capitol Hill food crawl at MATCHBOX with their unlimited brunch. They have a large selection of dishes and pizzas to choose from, but drinks come at an additional cost. Signature bloodies, bubblies, and cocktails are an extra $10.50 each, but they have 3 standard brunch cocktails (mimosas, peach Bellinis, and Bloody Marys) available for $3 with the purchase of their all-you-can-eat deal.

Their must-try plates are as follows: shrimp and grits; arancini; fire and smoke pizza; and lemon pound cake french toast. The shrimp is succulent, and the cheddar grits are just the right amount of rich. The andouille sausage adds great flavor, and the butter sauce is a decadent touch. Their arancini is among the best in the capital so indulge whether you go for brunch, lunch, or dinner. Each crispy ball is filled with cheesy risotto and served in a light marinara.

Matchbox is known for their pizza and for good reason. The fire and smoke is one of their signatures, and it's topped with chipotle purée, roasted garlic, onions, red peppers, smoked gouda, and basil. They use a very spicy sauce on top so expect some heat. Dessert isn't included on the menu, but options like cinnamon rolls and lemon pound cake french toast satisfy any and every sweet tooth. The latter's topped with blackberry Riesling sauce, fresh

Matchbox on Capitol Hill focuses on fresh, house-made pizzas wood-fired in a custom hand-built oven. We make everything, from our daily rotating soups to our double-chocolate chip brownie in-house and we are proud of it! We take to heart our motto, "the food is only as good as the hands that prepare it," and empower our chefs and team members to do anything that it takes to cause our guests to return time after time.

—Jim Drost, culinary director

strawberries, and salted almond streusel. It's very well balanced, and the cake's light and moist. The atmosphere's energetic, and this restaurant's always bustling. Make reservations to avoid waiting and enjoy live jazz on Sunday.

THE GEORGETOWN CRAWL

1. **DISTRICT DOUGHNUT,** 3327 Cady's Alley NW, (202) 333-2594, districtdoughnut.com

2. **DOG TAG BAKERY,** 3206 Grace St. NW, (202) 527-9388, dogtagbakery.com

3. **AMERICA EATS TAVERN,** 3139 M St. NW, (202) 450-6862, americaeatstavern.com

4. **BAKED & WIRED,** 1052 Thomas Jefferson St. NW, (202) 333-2500, bakedandwired.com

Georgetown

The Dough-pest Desserts

GEORGETOWN IS ARGUABLY THE MOST BEAUTIFUL neighborhood in DC. Situated along the Potomac River, this historic district's known for its cobblestone walkways, impressive shopping scene, and diverse food selection. There are over 100 restaurants in the area, so there's a lot to choose from. No worries though: That just means you'll have to make multiple trips back to experience it all.

Rent a kayak at the Key Bridge Boathouse or walk along the Chesapeake and Ohio Canal to work up an appetite. Or indulge in some well-deserved retail therapy on M Street because #treatyourself. They have everything from high-end boutiques like Alice & Olivia to cool second-hand shops like Ella Rue so shop like there's no tomorrow. You also can't leave without exploring Dumbarton Oaks, a 27-acre historic park that'll make you feel like you walked straight into your favorite rom-com. Then walk down to the waterfront to cool down with their sprinkler water fountain and feed the ducks before embarking on your massive dessert crawl.

1

DISTRICT DOUGHNUT

DISTRICT DOUGHNUT is happiness in a box. Hidden within the cobblestone walkways of Cady's Alley, this little slice of dessert heaven will bring you all the joy with the smell of freshly brewed coffee and caramelized sugar. Everyone hypes them up, but they fully live up to their very high reputation. They have some of the best doughnuts in the capital, and they're made from scratch daily so you know you're getting the freshest noms possible all day every day. They change flavors seasonally, so there's always something new to try. However, bestsellers like Brown Butter and Vanilla Bean Crème Brûlée are available year-round, so don't fret.

> We want to create a place where people find happiness—even if just for a moment. We believe that it's possible through something as classic, timeless, and delicious as a doughnut and coffee. Hopefully, we can make your day a little bit better when you step inside our stores.
>
> —Will Hand, co-owner

Their showmanship's on point, too. If you get a crème brûlée doughnut, they'll torch it for you on the spot, so make sure you have your camera ready! Your first bite will give you chills—that crackly crust is unlike any other, and it's so scrumptious you'll be tempted to get a second.

They have locations all over DC, so if you can't get to the store in Georgetown, Capitol Hill, Union Market, and the Wharf are options as well. Remember to go early though because their doughnuts sell out ridiculously fast!

2 DOG TAG BAKERY

This DC staple is a must for those of you looking to indulge in some solid baked goods. Located next to the canal near the Waterfront, DOG TAG BAKERY is a spacious cafe and the ideal place to grab coffee with friends or catch up on work. Their patriotic decorations are charming—remember to snap a picture of their dog tag chandelier—and the bakery has a very welcoming feel to it.

They're known for their cookies and cake, but they have a wide array of pastries and sandwiches that will do your tummy good. Their chocolate chip and ginger snap cookies are crispy on the outside, and soft and chewy on the inside. The chocolate mousse layer cake is delicious as well. It's extremely decadent without being overwhelmingly sweet, and it's moist with tons of mousse and frosting. The Oreo cream pie is another fan favorite, so make sure you grab a slice to go.

To further sweeten the pot, they're passionate about giving back to the community. With a hashtag like #bakingadifference, how could you not support this local business? Their 5-month fellowship program helps service-disabled veterans, military spouses, and caregivers gain the

knowledge and experience they need to find fulfillment in their personal and professional lives. Awesome, right? Their participants get hands-on training at their bakery and take relevant courses at Georgetown University, so they're business ready by the end. Their graduates have gone on to start their own businesses, continue their education at world-class universities, and take positions with top employers. So, do your part and go eat for a cause!

3 AMERICA EATS TAVERN

José Andrés can do no wrong, and **AMERICA EATS TAVERN** is a testament to that statement. The tavern is known for its barbecue and impressive selection of whiskey, but their desserts are up there as well so remember to save room post meal. You'll be tempted by all their carefully curated sweets, but standouts are their Chicago-style cheesecake and their warm chocolate cookie pie.

Both desserts are assembled right at your table, so have your phone ready because it makes for a fun Instagram story. The cheesecake is as creamy as can be, and it's placed on top of a delicious graham cracker crumble. Then, it's finished off with fresh raspberry sauce. The cookie pie is baked to order so expect to wait a good 10 to 15 minutes before you can dig in. It's truly worth the wait though. This epic cake-like-cookie is served piping hot with house-made bourbon vanilla ice cream, sea salt, and macerated berries. It's big enough to share with friends—if you're feeling really generous.

Also, remember to come back for brunch service, because they have some of the best waffles in DC. You can't go wrong with their chicken and waffles, or waffles and berries. Their egg sandwich is also really good, and their hush puppies could end wars.

4 BAKED & WIRED

Words can't begin to express the goodness that is **BAKED & WIRED**. Expect a wait regardless of the time or day because everyone (and their mom) loves the obscenely large cupcakes. Service is fast though, so don't fret if you see a line out the door! There's seating in the back, but the space itself is fairly cramped because they're a small hole-in-the-wall establishment that's family run. Note: They have tables outside so that's always an option if weather permits.

They bake in small batches to ensure quality, and they have some crazy creative flavors like Almond Orangesicle, Dirty Chai, and Phat Mint Oreo. The frosting to cake ratio is always balanced, and their coffee game is strong as well. They carry joe from reputable roasters like Intelligentsia, Mountain Air, and Elixir, so make sure you grab a cup to complement your sweets.

On top of nom cupcakes, they sell quiche, brownies, ice cream sammies, biscotti, and other delicious treats. They also have some pretty incredible gluten-free and vegan options, so feel free to take all your friends and family. This one of a kind bakery is an absolute must-try, so head on over to splurge on the best cupcake you'll ever taste. You're welcome in advance.

> Don't forget to check out their sister restaurant, Baked Joint (440 K St. NW). They are known for their house-made sandwiches and pizza, so make sure you stop by for lunch or dinner.

THE LOGAN CIRCLE CRAWL

1. THE PIG, 1320 14th St. NW, (202) 290-2821, thepigdc.com

2. BAAN THAI, 1326 14th St. NW, (202) 588-5889, baanthaidc.com

3. CHURCHKEY, 1337 14th St. NW, (202) 567-2576, churchkeydc.com

4. DOLCEZZA GELATO & COFFEE, 1418 14th St. NW, (202) 817-3900, dolcezzagelato.com

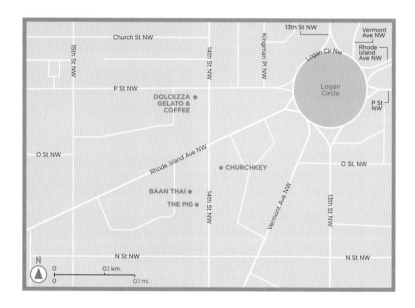

Logan Circle

Food So Sexy It'll Stop Traffic

WITH A PLETHORA OF INDIE STORES, HIP RESTAURANTS and fresh entertainment, the Logan Circle area—named for General John Logan, whose statue graces the traffic circle that gives the neighborhood its name—has an eclectic vibe to it. Start your adventure off at Miss Pixie's Furnishings & Whatnot. It's a DC favorite with antiques and second-hand items that appeal to people of all ages. Remember to grab a fresh cookie by the register to give you that extra oomph of energy before you start your shopping extravaganza!

Then, head to Studio Theatre to catch a contemporary performance that will seriously wow. There are four halls on location, and each space seats less than 225 people for an intimate experience you won't easily forget. Founded by Joy Zinoman, the institution's been around for 41 years, and they present a wide range of works, showcasing their immense versatility.

Black Cat's yet another great option for live entertainment. They've been around since the early '90s, and they feature a lot of up-and-coming indie artists. Pay to see the mainstage concert or hang out on ground level for free and hit up their game machines for a nostalgic night out. If you prefer something a bit more mainstream, they have regular DJ sets as well. For more arcade games, head to Players Club to satisfy your inner child. They also have foosball and pool as well, so enjoy some friendly competition with your friends before embarking on your food adventure.

1 THE PIG

Meat lovers rejoice! Located on 1320 14th Street, **THE PIG** sources their ingredients from their farm in La Plata, Maryland. They pride themselves on celebrating the animal in its entirety and serve up pork in every which way, even utilizing parts like the tail.

Their waitstaff is always accommodating, and the space has a casual but warm atmosphere. The restaurant has an impressive menu with several enticing options, but they're best known for their face bacon. Think of this fatty cut as a thick slice of heaven. The meat's very tender, and it's served with rosemary maple and cognac mustard—the former adds a subtle sweetness to the dish which cuts through beautifully.

Their pork belly buns are yet another must. They're braised master-fully and served with pickles, which add a lovely crunch. The protein's extremely flavorful, and the toasted buns add wonderful texture to the umami explosion. Other standouts include their *chilaquiles* and their applewood-smoked ribs. *Chilaquiles* is a traditional Mexican dish, and their take contains corn chips tossed with charred tomatillo salsa, queso fresco, and crema, which is then topped with a sunny-side up egg. The flavors are spot on, and it's one of the strongest brunch entrees you can get in the capital. The ribs are a popular dinner option, and they come with a side of freshly cut fries and celeriac slaw. They use Memphis dry rub on the meat and douse it in Dr Pepper barbecue sauce for a sweet and spicy finish. The meat falls right off the bone, and you can either get a half or whole rack.

2

BAAN THAI

This DC gem is a humble establishment with simple decor but killer food. Located on the second floor—ironically above another Thai restaurant—BAAN THAI offers traditional northern-style cuisine, so don't expect to find pad thai or drunken noodles here. The restaurant has a casual ambiance, and the space is flooded with light. Service is always quick, and the pricing is affordable.

They have a variety of Thai and Japanese dishes available, but stick with the former. Their sushi is fine, but their Thai food is exceptional. The food is rich in flavor, and they're not afraid to crank up the heat so remember to keep a glass of milk nearby. Must-try appetizers include their *tŭng tohng*, golden fried pockets, and their *saa-kuu sâi gài*, tapioca dumplings. The former contains ground chicken and shrimp, and it's wrapped in a thin rice paper, which is then deep fried and served with a side of sweet chili sauce. The tapioca dumplings are filled with ground chicken, garlic, and peanuts, and they're topped with sliced peppers. The chicken mixture's delicious, but it's the texture that's spectacular. It's just the right amount of chewy!

For entrees, get their *guuai-dtiiao tom yum*, a type of noodle soup, and their *khao soi gài*, yellow curry egg noodles. The tom yum's fresh and light, and it contains rice noodles, roasted pork, ground chicken, crispy pork skin, and a handful of other vegetables. It's a wonderful balance of sour, spicy, and hot! The *khao soi gài*, on the other hand, is an explosion of texture. The juiciness of the chicken, the crunchiness of the crispy egg noodles, and the richness of the curry all come together to create a symphony of deliciousness. End on a high note with an order of their coconut griddles!

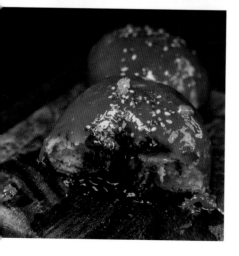

3

CHURCHKEY

Located above Birch & Barley, **CHURCHKEY** has a low-lit atmosphere that's intimate and romantic. With over 500 bottles of beer, an impressive wine list, and craft cocktails, this establishment is drink heaven. Beer director Greg Engert offers a wide range of styles and flavors with varying price points. "One of the keys to our program is that we balance traditional styles with more contemporary innovations, being sure to have

I hope that guests have an experience when they visit ChurchKey. Our outstanding staff will engage and guide our guests through our deep beer list, finding that perfect brew and touching on all of the things that make that selection so special. They will then dive into our food menu to get the very best dishes to create pairings for each and every beer selected. Throughout it all, I hope that our guests feel at home at ChurchKey and that they can count it as a great bar, first and foremost, and one they'd love to frequent.

—Greg Engert, partner and beer director at Neighborhood Restaurant Group

something suited to every palate and every plate that comes out of our kitchen," Engert says.

Although ChurchKey is a beer aficionado's dream come true, the food's on point as well. Chef Jarrad Silver and his culinary team provide classic American favorites with an imaginative twist, and bar food has never tasted better. They do everything from flatbreads to tot poutines, and with dishes like chicken pot pie croquettes and duck confit fritters, they hit it out of the park every time.

Must-try bites include their harissa wings, whole roasted cauliflower, and sea baked oysters. Everything's tasty, but make a note to try their cauliflower. It doesn't sound particularly exciting on paper, but the flavors are extraordinary. It's served with *muhammara* and shallot vinaigrette, then sprinkled with sesame seeds. The oysters are topped with roasted garlic breadcrumbs and a harissa butter, and the wings have a beautiful kick thanks to Chef Jarrad's special glaze.

DOLCEZZA

GELATO

ESPRESSO
VANILLA BEAN
PEPPERMINT STRACCIATELLA
DARK CHOCOLATE
MILK CHOCOLATE
THAI COCONUT MILK
MASCARPONE & BERRIES

BLACKBERRIES & CREAM
CARAMEL
ACCIATELLA

SORBETTO

YELLOW PEACH
SOUTHERN COMFORT

LEMON OPAL BASIL

PINEAPPLE HONEY LIME

MOJITO

BLUEBERRY LEMON
THYME

CHAMPAGNE MANGO

OXBLOOD PLUM

PINT 8.00
PUSH POP 4.00

AFFOGATO 6.50
ESPRESSO W/ GELATO

OUR FARMERS

OPAL BASIL LEMONADE

4 DOLCEZZA GELATO & COFFEE

DOLCEZZA GELATO & COFFEE was first established in 2004. They're famous for their freshly spun gelato and sorbets, and they source all their ingredients from local farms to keep things fresh. Their cafe's small, but their interior's beautiful and it's a wonderful place to recharge. Their menu changes frequently based on what's available, so sampling's encouraged. Get a small to enjoy 2 flavors and a large for 3. Popular gelato options include their dark chocolate and black sesame, and they're as rich and creamy as can be. Prefer something a little lighter? Their sorbets are refreshing and delightful. They always have creative flavors on hand, so opt for something unique.

They're also known for their coffee, so get a cup to enjoy with your dessert. They work closely with Sey Roasters and offer 4 single-origin coffees in addition to a wonderful decaffeinated option. They get fresh beans each week and use different brewing methods for variety. For espresso, they use Hunapu beans, grown in Antigua, Guatemala, because their subtle chocolate and hazelnut undertones complement their beverage offerings effortlessly. They have locations all over the greater DC area including Dupont Circle, CityCenter, and the Wharf.

THE CLEVELAND PARK CRAWL

1. SIAM HOUSE, **3520 Connecticut Ave. NW, (202) 363-7802,** siamhousedc.com

2. BYBLOS DELI, **3414 Connecticut Ave. NW, (202) 364-6549,** byblosdc .com

3. FIREHOOK BAKERY, **3411 Connecticut Ave. NW, (202) 362-2253,** firehook.com

4. VACE ITALIAN DELICATESSEN, **3315 Connecticut Ave. NW, (202) 863-1999,** vaceitaliandeli.com

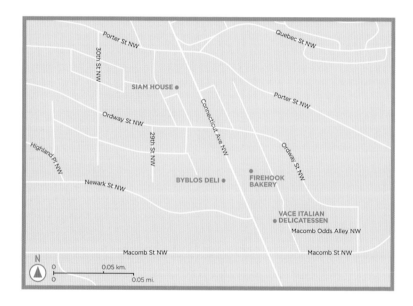

Cleveland Park

Suburban Charm at Its Finest

CLEVELAND PARK'S KNOWN FOR ITS CHARMING ATMOSPHERE, and it's a remarkable example of nature meets urban. It was a "streetcar suburb" back in the 1890s, when streetcar lines gave DC residents easy access to jobs in the city and led to the residential area's development. The neighborhood was named after President Grover Cleveland because he built a summer home there during his term in the late 19th century. Back then, they also called it Cleveland Heights and Connecticut Avenue Highlands, but those names didn't stick.

Find beautifully preserved Queen Anne–style homes and a charming commercial center that oozes small town vibes. Expect to see various types of architecture and enjoy the greenery if weather permits. If you're a nature-lover, schedule a hike or two at nearby Rock Creek Park. They have over 32 miles of trails available so there's much to explore. During the summer, they have live entertainment at their Carter Barron Amphitheater, so pack some snacks and make a day trip out of it.

Don't forget to visit the Smithsonian National Zoo while you're there. Admission is free, and it's home to over 1,500 creatures including exotic animals like pandas and African elephants. They also have cool events scheduled for both adults and kids, so keep an eye on their schedule to take advantage of everything they have to offer. Wear sneakers because you'll be walking quite a bit, which counters all the splurging you're going to do afterwards.

1

SIAM HOUSE

In the mood for some delicious Thai food? Well, you're in luck, because Cleveland Park's crawl starts off at **SIAM HOUSE**. This charming restaurant serves quality food that will light your taste buds on fire. The space is small but inviting, and they have a fairly large patio for those who prefer to dine outside.

Their menu has classic favorites like pad thai along with chef specials like wild tilapia and *moo-ping*. Whether you're craving curries or traditional noodle dishes, Siam House has everything you could possibly want. Start your meal off with an order of their *larb gai*, Thai curry puffs, or spring rolls. These are three of their most popular appetizers so you can't go wrong with any! They're heavy handed with their fish sauce though so their *larb*—minced chicken that's mixed with spices and lime juice—is especially pungent. Enjoy it with a side of rice for a filling meal or share with friends for a flavorful beginning.

In terms of entrees, they do drunken noodles and *moo-ping* extremely well. You can get the former with fried tofu, chicken, pork, beef, shrimp, or seafood, and it's the epitome of chewy awesomeness. The seasoning's always on point, and the spice level is just right. The *moo-ping*'s traditional Thai street food at its finest. It's marinated grilled pork that's served with sticky rice and steamed vegetables. The meat's as succulent as can be, and it tastes even better when dipped in the accompanying sauce. Just remember to save room, because their mango sticky rice dessert is bliss.

BYBLOS DELI

This Greek eatery is a local gem, so if you find yourself in Cleveland Park, you need to try their food: no ifs, ands, or buts. Chef Marc Adas offers budget-friendly eats 7 days a week so you'll most definitely see him behind the counter when you go. It's a hole-in-the-wall kind of establishment, so it's a great place to

grab casual bites. His menu boasts Mediterranean classics along with a handful of American standards, but don't be tempted by the latter. Cheeseburgers are great and all, but this is not the time nor place to indulge.

The Byblos Special is the most expensive item on their menu at $8.95, but the entree size is generous so it could easily make two meals. Get your choice of grilled chicken, kafta, or gyro meat on rice with big dollops of hummus and tzatziki along with a half pita. If you want something a bit more portable, get chef's chicken shawarma. It's a huge pita that's stuffed with the juiciest marinated chicken, and it also contains garlic, tomatoes, and tahini sauce.

Everything's made to order so food comes out piping hot, and they have daily specials available so make sure you take a look. Round your meal off with some of their baklava—think sweet, flaky goodness that will leave you wanting more.

3 FIREHOOK BAKERY

Although **FIREHOOK BAKERY** is known for their crackers and artisanal bread, they do sweets just as well, if not better. This welcoming coffee shop has been offering beautiful desserts since 1997, and they now have several other locations in the DelMarVa area. It's hard not to get one of everything from their stunning display, but must-trys include their bittersweet chocolate and key lime tarts. Both are standouts—they're beautifully presented, and they taste as delectable as they look. They bake everything fresh daily, so you'll experience quality in each mouthwatering bite. Their cookies are also exceptional—not to mention massive—and local favorites include sugar and chocolate chip.

Indoor seating is fairly limited, but they have a lovely garden out back with several tables and chairs. It's arguably one of the best patios in Cleveland Park, so plan to spend some time here whether you're alone or hanging out with loved ones. Everything is priced reasonably, so expect great bang for your buck! And if you're in the mood for something savory, they have hearty breakfast and lunch options available—think stuffed croissants, fresh quiche, loaded salads, and more.

4   VACE ITALIAN DELICATESSEN

Founded by Blanca and Valerio Calcagno, VACE ITALIAN DELICATESSEN has been serving DC since 1976. This quaint deli makes more than 60 items in-house and offers everything from mushroom truffle pâté to fresh squid ink pasta. However, they're most famous for their amazing pizza and ginormous cold cut sandwiches.

They have over 20 different deli meats available, and you have a choice between Italian bread or fresh house-made focaccia. They're very generous with their fillings, so keep your expectations high. To further sweeten the pot, their sandwiches are well under $10, and portions are huge so both your stomach and wallet will leave satisfied.

Their pies are spectacular as well. In fact, many would argue that they have some of the best pizza in the District. The crust is simple and has a lovely smokiness to it. The marinara sauce they use is layered on top of the cheese, and it has a surprising kick. You can keep things simple and eat it plain, or top your pie with quality ingredients like sopressata salami, sundried tomatoes, pancetta, and prosciutto. Their pizza freezes well so don't

worry about leftovers, but if you just want to sample a slice or two, you can order pieces individually. This is strictly a carryout joint, so enjoy your food outside if weather permits. And make sure you get a cannoli to go as well!

THE PARK VIEW CRAWL

1. **CALL YOUR MOTHER DELI**, 3301 Georgia Ave. NW, callyourmotherdeli
    .com

2. **HEAT DA SPOT CAFÉ**, 3213 Georgia Ave. NW, (202) 836-4719,
    heatdaspot.com

3. **NUVEGAN CAFÉ**, 2928 Georgia Ave. NW, (202) 232-1700,
    ilovenuvegan.com

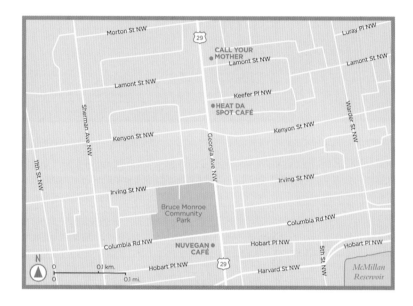

Park View

Eclectic Eating on Georgia Avenue

LOCATED NORTH OF HOWARD UNIVERSITY, PARK VIEW is a quiet yet friendly neighborhood. It's a developing area, but it's home to several mom and pop shops that'll make you feel like home. With everything from Jewish bagels to incredible Ethiopian food, you'll find yourself liking it more and more with each visit. It's a thriving community with supportive patrons that want to see local business prosper.

Looking to enjoy a show before you embark on your food crawl? Head to Story District for compelling performances that'll feed both your mind and soul. Previously known as SpeakeasyDC, they often collaborate with other groups and bring in acts from all around the country to diversify their lineup.

Prefer to bask in nature and spend your time outdoors? Head to Bruce Monroe Park. This lovely community space has everything from basketball courts to a large communal garden, and there are two playgrounds available so it's especially appealing for families with children. Afterwards, walk to the Midlands Beer Garden to sip local brews while munching on pre-crawl snacks. They have over 6,000 square feet of indoor and outdoor space, and they're pet friendly so what's not to like? Go during happy hour to get BOGO drafts. Here's to pre-gaming before you indulge in a fantastic crawl!

1

CALL YOUR MOTHER DELI

Where else in DC can you enjoy incredible bagel sandwiches with '90s hip-hop playing in the background? Decorated with photos of Drake, **CALL YOUR MOTHER DELI** is a Jewish deli and a newer addition to Park View. They offer non-traditional menu items like pastrami fried rice and pizza bagels, and they source ingredients from local suppliers like Z&Z and Ivy City Smokehouse to keep things fresh.

They have 8 different bagel sandwiches available, but customization is an option as well. Popular bites include their Rihanna-flex, their Shyne, and their latkes.

The Rihanna-flex is an everything bagel slathered with cream cheese then topped with smoked salmon, cucumbers, tomatoes, onions, and capers. They're generous with their fillings, and their bagels are everything a good bagel should be. They're made on site daily so expect soft, chewy goodness that will hit the spot every time.

The Shyne is the ultimate breakfast sandwich, packed with bacon or pastrami, bodega-style egg, American and cheddar cheeses, and spicy honey. It's also served on an everything bagel, but you can swap it for something else. The following 5 varieties are available daily until they sell out: plain, sesame, everything, za'atar, and chocolate. The za'atar is exceptionally delicious, and it works with either of the aforementioned sandwiches. As for sides, their crispy latkes are packed with flavor and served with jam, but they're scrumptious with or without the accompanying spread.

They also have wonderful vegetarian options like the Mila, a za'atar bagel topped with hummus, spicy sunflower seeds, and a seasonal vegetable salad. They pride themselves on quality, so get a bagel or 5, and enjoy the vibrant, whimsical interior to start your crawl with a bang.

2 HEAT DA SPOT CAFÉ

Located on Georgia Avenue, this hidden gem is a family-run business that goes above and beyond to make sure their customers leave full and satisfied. **HEAT DA SPOT CAFÉ**'s interior is eclectic, much like their menu. There's a broad range of dishes to choose from, but their Ethiopian fare reigns supreme. Everyone at this neighborhood mom and pop joint will make you feel right at home. The space is small but inviting, and there's plenty of seating outside on their patio as well. The vibe's laid back, and the quirky decor's charming.

Start off with their Ethiopian-style breakfast. It's a vegetarian dish with scrambled eggs, sauteed vegetables, and a myriad of seasonings. It's served with injera, and you eat it with your fingers. The bread has a spongy texture to it, and it's traditionally made with teff flour. Tear off a small piece, grab some scrambler, and enjoy. Douse it in their house "secret sauce" to add kick to an already spicy dish. It adds a fair amount of heat and a whole lot of flavor. They're also known for their sandwiches, and portions are huge so expect leftovers. First-timers get coffee on the house, and on Sunday, they have an Ethiopian buffet available all day.

3

NUVEGAN CAFÉ
With three locations in the DelMarVa area, NUVEGAN CAFÉ (previously known as Everlasting Life Cafe) is a family-run business that provides incredible vegan soul food that will leave one's taste buds completely and utterly satisfied. Their cafeteria-style kitchen is as efficient as can be. On top of serving delicious food, they're a socially responsible restaurant that constantly looks for ways to give back. They support various city initiatives to reinvest in the community they love so much.

There's a lot to choose from, but their staff's super friendly, and they encourage their customers to sample whatever they want before placing an order so don't be shy. Their food is great for vegans and carnivores alike, and this fast-casual joint has a laid-back vibe that's appealing for people of all ages.

Standout dishes include their crab cakes and their black bean burgers. Their "crab" is made with soy protein, and it's served with 2 sides of your choice and a delicious cream dipping sauce. The mac and cheese is phenomenal, but the garlic kale and mung bean are also delicious. There's a wide range of freshly prepared options to choose from, so get whatever your heart desires. Entree portions are big enough to share if you're feeling generous, but most likely you'll want to save leftovers for another meal.

Index

About Nomtastic Foods

What up, guys! I'm **DR. KIMBERLY KONG**, and I'm a Juilliard-trained pianist and teacher by day and dedicated blogger by night. On top of posting drool-worthy food porn, I write about glam living on a budget on **SENSIBLE STYLISTA**, my lifestyle blog. It's my mission in life to help you all live like royalty without breaking the bank, so make sure you follow along.

'Suuup, world! I'm **ROBBY MYERS**, and I was born and raised in San Francisco, California, with a five-year stint in SoCal and a couple years in Tokyo. I'm an avid adventurer in search of all things delicious and love finding hidden gems all over. When I'm not balancing six tacos in one hand with a camera in the other, I'm all about traveling, travel photography on my other Instagram account (Scenic Path),

body weight exercises, cruising down Highway 1, and producing and writing my own hip-hop music in English and Japanese.